THE SOUL OF SUPERVISION
INTEGRATING PRACTICE AND THEORY

Margaret Benefiel and
Geraldine Holton, editors

 Morehouse Publishing

NEW YORK · HARRISBURG · DENVER

Unless otherwise noted, the Scripture quotations contained herein are from the New Revised Standard Version Bible, copyright © 1989 by the Division of Christian Education of the National Council of Churches of Christ in the U.S.A. Used by permission. All rights reserved.

Morehouse Publishing, 4775 Linglestown Road, Harrisburg, PA 17112

Morehouse Publishing, 445 Fifth Avenue, New York, NY 10016

Morehouse Publishing is an imprint of Church Publishing Incorporated.
www.churchpublishing.org

Cover art courtesy of Thinkstock

Cover design by Christina Moore

Library of Congress Cataloging-in-Publication Data

The soul of supervision: integrating practice and theory / Margaret Benefiel and Geraldine Holton, editors.
    p. cm.
  Includes bibliographical references and index.
  ISBN 978-0-8192-2376-0 (pbk.)
  1. Supervision. I. Benefiel, Margaret. II. Holton, Geraldine.
  HM1253.S68 2010
  260.68'3--dc22
                        2010017968

Printed in the United States of America

Contents

Part I

Reflective Practice

Part II

Theories, Models, and Frameworks

Part III

Integrating Practice and Theory

Acknowledgments

First and foremost, we want to thank the contributors who made this book possible. We are grateful for your insights, your generosity, and your wide-ranging knowledge and experience. We are grateful to those of you who have taught with us in the Supervisory Practice program at the Milltown Institute in Dublin, to those of you who participated in the program, and to those of you who, as like-minded colleagues, slipped effortlessly into the flow of this book from your experience in other institutions. We feel fortunate to know you all, and to have the privilege of sharing the pages of this book with you.

We thank the Milltown Institute, who provided us with a grant to support our writing which helped us set aside time and space we would not have otherwise had. We owe a special thanks to the participants in the Supervisory Practice program, experienced adult learners who taught us at least as much as we taught them.

We are grateful to Nancy Fitzgerald who believed in this book from the beginning and brought it to Morehouse Publishing initially. Ryan Masteller, Dennis Ford, and Frank Tedeschi, the team at Morehouse who walked with us through the editing and production process, supported us beautifully. Your patience, encouragement, and careful attention to detail kept us moving and made this a much better book.

Finally, a special thanks goes to Michael Carroll, whose own work in the field of supervision as a trainer and writer has been pioneering. His foreword reflects the breadth and depth of his experience and his innovative approach to supervision as he continues to lead the way in this emerging profession.

Foreword

About five years ago I was privileged to be asked by Maoris in New Zealand to spend a weekend on their Marae helping them articulate what Maori supervision might mean for them. All forty Maoris were helping professionals—psychologists, social workers, probation officers, counselors, psychotherapists and youth workers—and all had a similar great yearning that supervision be integrated into their Maori culture. They shared the experience of having to submit to supervision that belonged to other races and cultures and felt that they had yet to give it a Maori flavor and context. Eventually they came up with a description of what Maori Supervision could mean: *"For us Maoris, supervision is gathering the treasures of the past into the competencies of the present for the wellbeing of the future"* (they had beautiful Maori words to capture the phrases "treasures of the past," "competencies of the present," and "wellbeing of the future"). This definition encompassed their close connection to their ancestors and to the traditions of the past while focusing on the needs of the present and preparing themselves for the future as professional workers. The rest of the time I shared with them was spent moving this philosophy of supervision into the practice of supervision and what that might mean in a Maori tradition: how supervision would include dancing and singing, eating food, and involve their incredible sense of how to be present in the here and now while connecting closely to the traditions of the past, particularly the presence of their ancestors.

You are probably wondering why I am recounting this story. After reading the various chapters in this new book on supervision, I sense that Ireland is on a similar journey to the Maoris—in this case, how to make supervision Irish. This is not the first book to be written in Ireland (or at least partially in Ireland) on supervision, but as far as I know it's the first book that begins to untangle what Irish supervision might mean. Where else would you find a book entitled, *The Soul of Supervision*, except in Ireland where the "soul" has such a lively history?

Its eleven chapters head straight for spirituality, spiritual direction, transformational learning, spiritual leadership, reflection, and emotional containing, as well as useful ways of engaging in supervision such as journaling and metaphor. Its "spiritual component grounds and surrounds the experience of supervision" as the authors of the introduction writes about the training course that inspired the book.

True, all the chapters are not written by Irish contributors: half the book comes from American authors. However, these authors have "clicked in" very neatly to the "soulful" and spirituality themes of the book and have given it an international flavor while retaining traditional themes of supervision. One of the authors recalls the Celtic tradition of heading off to sea and other lands in small boats without oars, and with only faith. This book does that too, metaphorically. While not as graphically stark as the sea-journey, the Irish-American connection speaks of that special relationship between the two countries. This book is undoubtedly a joint venture with the U.S. contributors, well-known and well-respected authors and specialists in their own right, especially in the field of pastoral supervision.

Of course, the problems with introducing or integrating spirituality into any professional format is that it can so easily narrow and restrict the work by focusing on one approach and come dangerously close to making one religious focus the meaning-maker for practice. To be asked to view your professional activities through the lens of religious tradition or a faith-wisdom (such as Christianity) will not sit easily with many people. There is still a strong reservation that if I engage in supervision with a supervisor who has a declared and definitive faith value then those values will be imposed at worst or at least unconsciously pervade the supervision room. This book, while unashamedly adopting a spirituality approach and one that is based in the Christian tradition, does not fall into that trap: rather the opposite in my view. It seeks to widen the discussion from a factual base (what is happening) to a meaning-making process that helps us read the facts or make sense of the facts through adopting a spiritual stance of wonder, awe, mystery, stopping, critical reflection, wisdom, contemplation, and stillness. One must not move too fast or too quickly and end up with impulsive answers. Supervision here wants to play with the facts— creatively, metaphorically, dialogically and cross-professionally. This is a book about how to make cross-professional supervision work without imposing one profession on the other but harnessing the best of both in the service of the work. It has words and phrases not commonly heard in the mainstream supervision literature: of supervision as vocation, a calling, a ministry; supervision as contemplative stance and faithful action, creating watchful hearts and moving toward becoming a "soulful supervisor." It's first and foremost about a philosophy of supervision— what supervision means, at heart. Secondly, it presents a theology of supervision which has at its center the theme of spirituality in its widest form. Thirdly, it zones in on pastoral supervision and pastoral ministry as a reflective methodology of thinking about supervision rather than an imposed value-set. Finally, *The Soul of Supervision* offers supportive interventions applicable across professions (such as dialogue, journaling, emotional containing and the use of metaphor).When Geraldine first asked me to write a foreword to this new book on supervision, I was flattered. It's always an honor to receive such a request. Besides the assumption that you have reached some credibility (maybe even gravitas) in the field in which the book is written, there is always the added honor of being placed alongside the author(s) as a peer. Living now in England, but having run an Advanced Diploma in Supervision which I directed and tutored in Ireland for a number of years, it was fascinating for me to realize the breadth and depth supervision has taken there more recently. Supervision in Ireland now has a distinctive international/diverse/Irish flavor. It wasn't so much that the immigrant called supervision was at last being naturalized in Irish soil—it was much more. The authors had dug deep into Irish culture and spirituality and given birth to the supervision that was waiting to be born. It was more than integration, more than a marriage; it was a rediscovery of how supervision had lain at the heart of Celtic life undiscovered for so long. Maybe the fact that it has been lost is partially to blame for some of the troubles besetting Ireland—when reflection, learning from experience, contemplation, spiritual leadership, transparency, and spirituality disappear or get lost then truly the soul of supervision has disappeared and undoubtedly the soul of the nation with it. Ireland has had a long traditional reputation for contemplation, closeness to nature, and—interestingly—connecting and combining traditions. That is why I think this book lives on the cusp of the future; it gives a hint to what can be when leadership, organizations, intentional thoughtfulness, and contemplation are used to stop and think deeply about what we are doing and from where within us our practice comes.

While there are many frameworks from which to make sense of supervision—for example, learning, philosophy, professional stances, and theoretical orientations—this book moves towards a spirituality mode from which to make meaning of experience. Sometimes that mode is quite direct when "faithful action" from the Scriptures is viewed as a flexible lens through which to make meaning. At other times the framework calls on spiritual themes as guides—for example, a sense of wonder, contemplative review, intentional reflective practice, provoking thoughtfulness, reverence, awe and privilege. The book calls for a "ministry of supervision" that is characterized by reflective and collaborative, cross-professional supervision. While the terminology is often spiritual (soul in contemplative stance, pastoral supervision, the ministry of supervision), it is never narrow in a religious or denominational sense.

This is a new book not just in the sense that it's hot off the presses. It's new also in that it begins to connect supervision and spirituality in an Irish and international context where diversity and cross-professionalism is the order of the day. As one of the authors puts it: it is supervision "beyond mind, beyond ego and beyond fear."

Michael Carroll
July 1, 2010

INTRODUCTION

෨ *Margaret Benefiel and Geraldine Holton* ෩

For nearly a decade, we have been teaching in a program in supervisory practice at the Milltown Institute (and now at All Hallows College)[1] in Dublin. The program, designed by Geraldine Holton, welcomes participants from various professions, including psychotherapists, pastoral counselors, spiritual directors, priests and ministers, chaplains, and educators. The contemplative tone, set early in the program, creates an invitational space for transformation.

We invite participants to bring their whole selves to the program: body, mind, heart, and soul. Through the collaborative learning group process (cohorts range from roughly 10 to 15 persons), participants build skills, learn theory, and experience deep transformation, learning in their bones a transformative model of supervision. Many participants find themselves drawn to the program because of its emphasis on soul; the spiritual component grounds and surrounds the experience.

The Soul of Supervision grew out of this supervisory practice program. With contributions by faculty in the program, participants, and other like-minded authors, the book invites readers into the transformative experience that program participants have had, and will invite program graduates into further transformation. The book also describes skills and examples of how those skills are used by practitioners of supervision in various ministries and professions.

Through the centuries, soul has been described in a wide variety of ways.[2] For Plato, for example, soul was the source of all change and transformation while for psychologist James Hillman, soul was the seat of calling, character and destiny. We believe that the soul of supervision is the contemplative stance within which the program and this book are grounded, the stance that leads not only to skill-building in an environment that is both safe and challenging, but also transformative. Soul finds expression in such qualities as authenticity, autonomy, decency, compassion, and sensitivity; and it is present in all actions that express integrity and ethical courage.

Brief History of Supervision

The field of management has contributed much to current images of supervision. Even Pharaoh, in building the pyramids, faced problems similar to those corporate executives face today, so supervision in some form stems from early human history. Contemporary management theory traces its roots to late in the nineteenth century and early in the twentieth century when Frederick Taylor (1856–1915) articulated his "scientific" theory of management. Taylor believed that workers needed to be coerced to work hard and viewed employees as means to the end of maximizing revenue.[3] Taylor's theory fit well with the rise of the theory of transactional leadership, which focused on rewards and punishments. In this understanding, the leader (or supervisor) holds the power and provides incentives for followers to do what the leader wants.[4] In contrast to the transactional approach, transformational leadership, articulated by James McGregor Burns[5] and Bernard Bass,[6] appealed to followers' better natures rather than relying on rewards and punishments. Transformational leaders (and supervisors) share a vision and inspire others to follow. In flatter or more person-centered organizations, supervisors often take the role of coaches or mentors, focusing on helping supervisees succeed in accomplishing their goals and in their development as professionals.[7]

Supervision in business and industry today reflects all these approaches and more, with the transactional approach, based on rewards and punishments, dominating.

At roughly the same time that Taylor began to develop the field of management science, the Charity Organization Society movement in New York formulated guidelines that became the basis of supervision in the newly-emerging profession of social work. In 1878 the Charity Organization Society began to oversee alms-giving practices by hiring agents to supervise volunteers. In both group and individual sessions, volunteers brought case studies which provided the material for supervision. By the turn of the century the basic components of contemporary social work supervision had been formulated.[8]

In the 1920's Sigmund Freud followed an apprenticeship model to introduce supervision of psychoanalysts in training, which led to clinicians bringing their client work to supervisors for discussion. By the beginning of the 1960s, the expectation in psychoanalytic circles was that psychoanalysts would receive 150 hours of supervision.[9]

In the field of education, supervision was introduced in schools to "maintain common standards of instruction" and to help in "deciding on the retention or promotion of individual teachers."[10] It quickly gained the appellation "Snoopervision." Between 1920 and 1950, two theories of educational supervision emerged. "Scientific supervision" emphasized the administrative and teaching functions of supervision. "Democratic supervision" stressed support and professional development for the teacher. The "democratic" approach has become the predominant approach in the field of education today.

Clinical Pastoral Education, developed by Anton T. Boisen (1876–1965) for hospital chaplains, drew on methods used in the supervision of psychotherapists and social workers and integrated a theological aspect. Boisen viewed theological reflection through the use of the verbatim and clinical case reports as studying "the living human document." Supervision of ministers in training built on the CPE model,[11] as did supervision of spiritual directors.[12]

Supervision has been recognized as a profession in its own right since the 1980s.[13] Supervision in its contemporary manifestation focuses on 1) ensuring that supervisees' clients are served well and 2) the supervisee's growth and development. Supervision is now being used in the professions of education, psychotherapy, ministry, social work, chaplaincy, spiritual direction, and nursing, among others.

The authors of this book draw primarily on understandings of supervision developed in the helping professions, viewing the supervisor as the supervisee's ally, helping supervisees grow, develop, and serve their clients well. While there will always be tension between the two functions of accountability and support, the authors of the following chapters seek to present theories and examples of supervision that focus on helping supervisees be their best selves, thus serving their clients (and the organizations in which they work) well, fulfilling both functions faithfully.

Structure of the Book

Part I focuses on supervision as reflective practice in a variety of settings. In chapter 1, Geraldine Holton sets the stage by using the metaphor of wisdom's garden to cultivate reflective practice in supervision across professions. In chapter 2, David McCormack explores journaling as self-supervision in an adult education setting. Chapter 3, by Debora Jackson, focuses on supervision as leadership development for ministerial students. In chapter 4, Martin McAlinden continues the focus on supervision in ministry by exploring ongoing supervision for priests. Yuko Uesugi, in chapter 5, elucidates a transformative approach to reflective practice in CPE supervision. Maureen Conroy, in chapter 6, presents a contemplative approach to supervising spiritual directors. In chapter 7, Margaret Benefiel explores supervision in organizations.

Part II moves from practice to theory, stepping back and formulating theories, models, and frameworks for understanding the reflective practices that were introduced in part I. Jack Finnegan, in chapter 8, explores a dialogical model for clinical supervision. Janet Ruffing extends the traditional contemplative model of supervision for spiritual directors in chapter 9, building on Barry Estadt's pastoral counseling model of supervision. Robert Moore presents a process model of supervision based on empathy in chapter 10.

Part III concludes the book with a dialogue between Robin Shohet, a pioneering leader in the field of supervision,[14] and Geraldine Holton, exploring the interplay between practice and theory.

It is our hope that these offerings will provide an invitation to explore the soul of supervision, for both supervisors and supervisees. We invite you to take a meta stance as you step into the pages of this book expectantly, open to transformation.

[1]The program is in transition from the Milltown Institute to All Hallows College. At the date of publication, the first cohort at All Hallows has begun at the same time that the last Milltown cohort is finishing its final year.

[2]For a detailed exploration of soul, see Jack Finnegan, *The Audacity of Spirit: The Meaning and Shaping of Spirituality Today* (Dublin: Veritas Publications, 2008), 209–234.

[3]Frederick Taylor, *The Principles of Scientific Management*, reprint of 1911 edition (Mineola, NY: Dover Publications, 1997).

[4]For a description of transactional leadership, see G. Yukl, *Leadership in Organizations*, 4th ed. (Upper Saddle River, NJ: Prentice Hall, 1998).

[5]J. M. Burns, *Leadership* (New York: Harper and Row, 1978).

[6]B. M. Bass, *Leadership Performance Beyond Expectations* (New York: Academic Press, 1985).

[7]See, for example, Southwest Airlines' model in M. Benefiel, *Soul at Work: Spiritual Leadership in Organizations* (New York: Seabury Books, 2005), 65–70.

[8]K. Pohly, *Transforming the Rough Places: The Ministry of Supervision*, 2nd ed. (Franklin, TN: Providence House Publishers, 2001), 53.

[9]B. D. Lewin and H. Ross, *Psychoanalytical Education in the United States* (New York, W. W. Norton, 1960), 257.

[10]R. L. Mosher and D. E. Purpel, *Supervision: The Reluctant Profession* (Boston: Houghton Mifflin, 1972), 18.

[11]See K. Pohly, *idem*.

[12]See chapter 9 of this book, in which Janet Ruffing discusses the origins of supervision in contemporary spiritual direction.

[13]E. Holloway, *Clinical Supervision: A Systems Approach* (London: Sage Publications, 1995).

[14]Robin Shohet co-authored with Peter Hawkins the highly-acclaimed *Supervision in the Helping Professions* 3rd edition (Oxford: Oxford University Press, 2006) and edited *Passionate Supervision* (London: Jessica Kingsley, 2007).

PART I

Reflective Practice

CHAPTER

1

∾

Wisdom's Garden:

A Metaphor for Cross-Professional Supervision Training

Geraldine Holton

B *eneath our educated and scholarly ways of knowing, another dynamic moves to explore the deep things of the person and to generate from hidden resources new, and sometimes powerful, insights that transform the horizons of intelligibility.*[1]

At a time when it is essential to model an approach to engagement in helping relationships which is accountable and based on firm ethical and professional foundations, the practice of regular supervision for those working in the caring professions is more important than ever. While this practice is commonplace in most clinical and counseling training contexts, no specific training program existed in Ireland to train practitioners in the skills of supervision for those working in the fields of pastoral care, adult education, spiritual direction, police force, health care professionals, chaplaincy, and organizations. Responding to the changing needs of practitioners, in 2002 I co-designed a Higher Diploma and Master's program in Supervisory Practice. These experiential and practice-based programs enable those in demanding professional helping relationships to identify and articulate a personal philosophy of supervision and to grow in their identity as cross-professional supervisors.

When designing the Supervisory Practice programs my vision was to create an environment for practitioners within an academic setting which could facilitate transformational learning and growth in wisdom. Many practitioners who train as supervisors carry with them the scars of previous negative academic experience and have developed a belief that they do not belong within this culture. My hope was to develop academic-practitioner collaboration. The journey has been a significant part of my personal and professional development over the past eight years. Holding the tension of two learning cultures, university and workplace, and meeting the demands of both has been a challenge that has been transformational.

What follows is a glimpse into that journey of transformation and the philosophy of supervisory practice that emerged from my research and practice. In this chapter I will focus on a specific application of practice and theory that I call "wisdom supervision," an approach to supervision based on wise collaborative conversation integrated with creative engagement with symbols. The following encounter illustrates the dynamic of "wisdom supervision" with a fictional supervisee named Kevin, an encounter which will be carried throughout the chapter.

Thank you for agreeing to meet with me for this supervision session. I don't really know where to start, maybe by saying that I am at a point in my practice when I feel that I want to do some further training but I am not sure what I need so I am hoping that this conversation might help me to know in what direction to go. My background is in psychotherapy and I have also been practicing as a trainer and an accredited supervisor for the past ten years. I feel I am a good supervisor and really enjoy this work but for me there is "something missing." I have taken part in many different supervisor training workshops and each time I have learned so much, but I am still searching for something. What it is I don't know. (Kevin sat silently with his unknowing before continuing.)

I picked up the brochure for the MA in Supervisory Practice and felt very drawn to it. I was not thinking of doing a Master's; I'm not an academic. I know you are Director of this program so maybe you can help. I think what caught me is the way the contemplative aspect is included. (Kevin became very uneasy, moving about in the chair.) I assume it is something to do with slowing down and reflecting. It's not that I'm a religious or spiritual person but there was something about this aspect of the program that struck me. It is something I have been thinking about for some time now. Recently, it has also come up in my client work. I don't talk about this in my practice, yet for me it is very important. I was wondering how I could begin to work with this part of myself without forcing it on the clients and supervisees I work with. It's like there is a part of me that I am not using, a part that may be helpful for clients. I am curious to hear more about this reflective aspect of the program. So could we focus on that in this session?

Personal-Professional Context

My professional work consists of research, training and practice in a psychotherapeutic and spiritual context, thus I use a psycho-spiritual interdisciplinary approach rooted in a contemplative, reflective, and social-constructionist philosophy.

My interest in supervision began during my training as a psychotherapist when as a supervisee I discovered that supervision is one of the main integrating processes for ongoing personal and professional development, and self-care as a helper. Thus began my passion for this area. Following the completion of an Advanced Diploma in Supervision with Michael Carroll, I based my developing model of supervision on Carroll's generic tasks.[2] Some years later I was invited to design and deliver a Higher Diploma and Master of Arts in Supervisory Practice program at Milltown Institute and more recently at All Hallows College, Dublin. I am currently engaged in doctoral research in supervision.

Like other professions, supervision has been influenced by the changing traditions and trends in society. In the past decade there has been an increasing emphasis upon collaborative practice and continuing professional development in the helping professions. One consequence of this has been the emergence of supervision as a profession in its own right. The closing decades of the twentieth century witnessed a growing interest in cross-professional supervision, in which trained supervisors from differing professional and disciplinary backgrounds supervise practitioners. In this context, more open and flexible approaches to training and accreditation in supervision are essential.

The Challenge of Definition

The task of defining supervision is complex. The term is used broadly to describe various arrangements such as line management or consultation. Perhaps the struggle to define supervision reflects a growing recognition of how complex the supervisory process is. Supervision provides a safe environment where both the practitioner and client are held. Supervision creates a container or transitional space for the emergence of a healthy selfhood, where all aspects of the self—

physical, spiritual, emotional, intellectual, personal, and professional—
are explored, reflected upon and integrated. It is a place where a personal
and professional identity is formed and transformed.

Reflecting on this holding environment in the supervisory space,
the *garden* surfaced for me as a root metaphor. Using symbols and
wise collaborative conversation in the creation of what I have named
"wisdom's garden" has become the foundation of a creative approach to
reflective practice in one-to-one and group supervision (see Figure 1).

Figure 1

Gardening, like supervision, is one of my passions and I see many
connections between gardening and supervision. When I am working
with the earth, tilling the soil of the supervisee, I can sense the enormous
responsibility of being a co-creator. As I silently finger the soil to plant
a bulb at just the right depth, in the right place at the right time, I
feel the intuitive promptings of the creative spirit and I sense the need
for mindful and contemplative presence. My mother was also an avid
gardener, and it was while kneeling in the clay beside this intelligent,
imaginative and innovative woman that many of the contemplative
and evocative skills of noticing, lingering, savouring, surrendering, and
waiting patiently were demonstrated for me. The contemplative aspect
within supervision is the act of cultivating a watchful heart, a reflective
presence, and observing without evaluation. When held in such an
environment, the supervisory experience can be truly restorative for

supervisees as they reconnect with the true self and grow in wisdom as they, in turn, hold the client.

Kevin is sitting in "wisdom's garden," a reflective, transformative space in which a new aspect of his identity emerges and he struggles to discover the way forward in his personal and professional journey. As Kevin honors his tacit knowledge and begins to discover the inner voice that is drawing him into the new, the seed-kernel of Kevin's wisdom awaits a wise gardener who will nurture it through wise conversation. I, as a generative listener and a good gardener, tend the new shoots that are slowly emerging, cultivating the new growth as it unfolds in a safe, holding environment. During this session and later when he participated in the Supervisory Practice training program, Kevin voices his openness to explore the newly emerging aspect of his identity and worldview.

It is important to view the self as emergent and changing as opposed to stable or fixed. Identity is formed by social processes and emerges from the dialectic between the individual and society.[3] Supervision can engender transformative learning in the struggle to construct a self-identity and a meaningful worldview. Establishing rapport, safety, and containment are important as Kevin begins to explore aspects of his professional identity and competence which might otherwise remain hidden and unexamined. Supervision provides a safe holding environment where, through wise conversation and creative attentiveness, individuals and groups can co-create a deeper perspective and wisdom that can lead to transformation and effective practice.

So what is this new identity that is emerging for Kevin through this wise conversation? How does he understand himself at this point as he continues to develop knowledge and clinical wisdom? Kevin is at the edge of his knowledge, his sense of self, and the world as he understands it. Being at the edge is an especially generative place to engage in supervision.

As Kevin and I continue our conversation, I invite him to use the metaphor of wisdom's garden as a way of reflecting together. Wisdom's garden is a helpful way of externalizing the supervisee's perception of an encounter, an event or a theme in which he feels challenged, unclear or unfree. Participation in this process is always invitational and responds to the needs of the supervisee and context. Kevin takes the opportunity to create a garden as a creative way of representing his dilemma, as the outer world connects with the inner world. Wisdom's garden helps to integrate experiential practice and theory. It is a holding space where the supervisee is free to explore on an intrapersonal level how their personal and professional identity and practice is changing, transforming and emerging. On the left side of his garden Kevin placed a small pile of books which symbolized the knowledge and experience he felt he had developed through his reflective practice, particularly through his practice of journaling. He represented his professional practice as a jigsaw puzzle with a piece missing, the missing piece representing the meaning-making aspect, the "something more" he had identified as missing. Beside the gap for the missing piece, he placed a bowl of sand which expressed how unfulfilled he felt at this moment in his practice and his growing desire to integrate a contemplative aspect into his work life. He identified this bowl of sand as a significant aspect of his garden (see Figure 2). I invited Kevin to rest in wisdom's garden with the creative tension of his confusion and uncertainty, hoping he might catch a glimpse of his own unique wisdom.

Figure 2

A Holding Environment

Kevin exemplifies the challenges of living in a postmodern world of flux and increasing pace where practitioners can become disconnected from their wise and authentic voices. Often the dream that originally drew practitioners into the work can lose its lustre within an environment that rewards productivity and individualism. There is a tendency to rush through the ever-expanding lists of tasks, doing the same thing over and over, only faster and faster, as a sense of meaninglessness and fragmentation develops. The supervisory process can enable supervisees to develop their professional identity and resolve any role confusion or sense of meaninglessness. If supervisees have not attained a sense of professional identity and vision, they may easily adopt the roles of other professionals. Modeling professional identity and an ease with uncertainty is an important part of the role of the supervisor.

Throughout the process with Kevin, I, as reflective witness, said very little. My task as supervisor was to facilitate reflection, thus helping Kevin to trust his own assessment of the situation even where it might be at odds with received wisdom. The ability to contain the process in silence and the principle of delayed interpretation augment the witness aspect. In this modality the role of the supervisor is that of holder of the space—including reflective witness, facilitator of meaning-making, and knowledge construction—through a quality of mindful presence, rather than knowledge bearer, expert, and problem solver. The integration of constructivist practices within wisdom supervision involves depth rather than breadth, process rather than product, and open-ended questioning techniques that require contemplation and reflection.

Constructivist learning is a dynamic process that requires the active engagement of the learner, rooted in a holistic stance towards knowledge and learning. For the supervisor it requires a flexible, negotiated, non-hierarchical way of being. When using wisdom's garden within group supervision, the group members are a supportive and reflective presence. The supervisee may, like Kevin, choose to remain silent, communicating non-verbally and symbolically. An effective supervisor is not afraid of silence. During the session with Kevin the pace was slow with long periods of silence as he stayed in tune with his internal supervisor, a term that captures reflection in action. The supervisory process is created *by* and *with* the supervisee rather than *for* and *to* them as supervisor and supervisee learn to approach each other with curiosity, openness, and anticipation.

Through my engagement in the MA program and a critical analysis of Michael Carroll's generic tasks of supervision, I affirm the necessity for supervisors to be skilled in the essential tasks of supervision as outlined by Carroll. However, within cross-professional supervision, another task, which I have named as the wisdom task, emerges. In supervision we each bring our own philosophy, gendered experiences, cultural and mental horizons—as well as our own spirituality and psychology—to bear in our efforts to reflect meaningfully on real situations. The wisdom task incorporates the meaning-making aspect of supervision. Wisdom's garden is an invitation into this space—the inner landscape of fear, hope, and imagination—to develop a resilient sense of at-homeness in oneself and a more authentic practice. Wisdom may, at least in part, be the missing piece Kevin is looking for as he engages at the intrapersonal level.

Transformational Learning

As any good gardener knows, an important part of preparing for planting seeds is to identify the type of soil in the garden, that is, in this case, the epistemological base or meaning-making framework. Once it is agreed that the supervisory relationship represents a reflective learning alliance, a well-grounded understanding of adult learning is a necessity within supervision. Thus, a key element informing the supervisory process and the training program is the application of the Transformational Learning Theory associated with Jack Mezirow,[4] which is based on the critical theory of Habermas.[5] A key role of an effective supervisor is to be a facilitator of learning.

An approach to adult learning that is based on transformational theory is influenced by constructivism, which sees learning as a dynamic process and contends that learners do not passively absorb information but construct new ideas or concepts with their current or past knowledge. The key insight of transformational learning theory, an appropriate name for this approach to knowledge making, is that we are all active constructors of knowledge who can become responsible for the procedures and assumptions that shape the way we make meaning.

Transformational learning means that individuals change their frames of reference; that is, they change the complex webs of assumptions, expectations, psychological characteristics, values, and beliefs that act as filters through which they view both themselves and the world in which they live. Transformational learning involves a deep shift in vision. According to Mezirow, this process usually begins with a "disorienting dilemma," a dissonant experience that contradicts our existing meaning perspective and related habits of mind such as the change in identity that Kevin is experiencing. A new awareness, centered around his lack of freedom to express the missing piece that is a much valued aspect of his practice, has provoked a change in Kevin's frames of reference, his vision.

As Kevin reflected on his garden it became clear to him that he could not ignore this gap, this missing piece. He was shocked by his lack of freedom to voice this desire even within his peer supervision group. "How has this happened?" he asked. Moving beyond ego and the desire for control, Kevin chose to face this dilemma as he critically reflected on his assumptions and lack of freedom.

The metaphor of a garden can be misunderstood to mean a place of bliss that has little connection with real life. However, while being a protected space, a garden, rather than being a place to retreat, can be a necessary holding environment for facing and engaging in life and its challenges in a powerful way. Supervision as reflective practice can become politically, socially, and psychologically challenging; it is a transformational rather than a quietist navel-gazing experience. The heart of the supervisory process is about challenging core beliefs which, if left unexamined, can keep one locked in society's paradigms. The role of the supervisor is to be a facilitator of change. When faced with a disorienting dilemma, supervisees may at first struggle, resisting the challenge. They may choose to ignore or avoid the dilemma and the change it may require, wishing to remain in their comfort zone. However, when ready to risk chaos, a disorienting event can, if they embrace it, be a catalyst for transformation. The paradox is that transformation is not possible without the accompanying chaos.

Reflective Process

A key strength of Mezirow's theory of reflectivity lies in the critical reflection process because it can lead to growth and transformation for the learner. He identifies three types of reflection: content, process and premise.[6] The first, "content reflection," is an examination of the content or description of the problem; the second, "process reflection," involves looking into the problem strategies that are being used; while the third, "premise reflection," can lead learners to a transformation of their meaning perspectives. Mezirow's six levels of reflection—affective, discriminant, judgmental, conceptual, psychic and theoretical—provide further focus and explanation of Kevin's inner experience.

As Kevin grappled with his unfreedom and engaged with the reflective process, he wondered why he had suppressed the contemplative dimension of himself, especially when he prized so highly his sense of freedom as a therapist and trainer. He also wondered how suppressing this dimension might have impacted his work with clients and trainees. Perhaps there was some parallel process here and his clients and trainees also felt blocked to voice this dimension of themselves. Could his block be blocking theirs? As I witnessed Kevin internalizing this block as a personal failure, I became alert to the role of the supervisor as facilitator of critical reflection. By embracing his own need for change, Kevin was also addressing critical issues within his practice and the wider profession which in time could transform the culture and shape the wider context.

Reflective practice is more than an examination of personal experience; it is located in the political and social structures. Like other professionals, supervisors seek to demonstrate a respect for diversity and to work knowledgeably and ethically with supervisees and clients who differ on many personal dimensions and worldviews, one such dimension being the supervisee's spiritual perspective. Because supervisors represent a powerful cultural group, they are challenged to develop more inclusive frames of reference and worldviews towards supervisees and clients with diverse belief systems.

Bernard and Goodyear[7] remind us that, in our roles as supervisors and practitioners, it is important to develop cultural competency skills and a level of comfort with difference. Through my experience with ANSE,[8] the European organization for supervisors, I have developed a new appreciation for diversity and difference. I have learned to perceive this diversity as an opportunity, evoking a sense of wonder rather than as a threat evoking fear and rigidity. The soulful supervisor learns to recognize, appreciate, and respond to diversity in a wise collaborative way. In their current research, Bernard and Goodyear identify the supervisee's spiritual perspective as an emerging, culturally determined subject of interest that has only recently surfaced in the supervision literature. For Kevin, the recognition of diversity, particularly in one's spirituality, is an important insight as he struggles to be more accepting of the cultural and personal differences he encounters in his practice. The importance of supervision as a safe holding environment is highlighted when it serves as an antidote to avoiding bringing such aspects as the contemplative, spiritual aspects of himself and his work into the light for critical reflection.

Within all caring encounters there is potentially a transcendent dynamic that encompasses yet lifts us beyond our professional skills and competencies into the realm of mystery. For some, this aspect is named spirituality, for others the mystery-mastery complex, but for me "wisdom" captures this in a cross-professional and psycho-spiritual context. This meaning-making task or wisdom task also challenges the supervisor to support supervisees as they develop their personal philosophies. How this aspect is named and integrated within cross-professional supervision is an area for further exploration and research. I believe it is time for supervisors and training programs to consider the inclusion of the spiritual perspective as an aspect of diversity, as they develop spiritual sensitivity and competency. Another important challenge for supervisors is to challenge hegemonic culture, such as the culture that Kevin is in, which is described by Brookfield[9] as a culture successful in persuading people "to consent" to their oppression.

Kevin included himself in the garden as a hill walker resting on a rock who, with all his knowledge in his backpack, looked across at two figures sitting together in the garden deep in conversation (see Figure 3). To the right of Kevin's garden, the grass was much greener! Kevin was quite moved as he sat in silence with this image. He said he felt a deep longing to connect with the two figures which for him symbolized his struggle to construct a self-identity and a more meaningful worldview that included a contemplative dimension. Speaking and listening with the language of symbols and silence, as well as the language of words, we were discovering and co-constructing this new meaningful worldview, a deep shift in vision.

Figure 3

Wisdom's Way of Knowing

I believe that Mezirow's emphasis on critical reflection in fostering transformative learning needs to be balanced by recognizing the role that was played during this session with Kevin by affective and other ways of knowing, such as symbolic literacy and spiritual intelligence. A more holistic approach that recognizes other ways of knowing, ways that are often neglected by the dominant academic discourse, is needed. The use of presentational or expressive ways of knowing, for example, invite the whole person into the learning environment, engaging the affective, intuitive, thinking, physical, and spiritual self. Drawing largely from the mystics and sages, Tobin Hart[10] offers a helpful map of knowing and learning that moves through six interrelated layers, including wisdom and the possibility of transformation. This holistic approach includes mind and heart, balances intuition with intellect, mastery with mystery, and cultivates wisdom instead of the mere accumulation of facts.

As already noted, critical reflection and transformational learning are key elements characterising supervisory practice in postmodern cultures. In my work I have come to appreciate the centrality of the wise, collaborative, and transformational learning dimensions of supervision. It is a dialogical, sharing process that surfaces the existence of alternative worldviews, uncovering the limitations of unexamined, habitual, and un-reflexive use of theories, beliefs, principles, or practices. At its best, the art of supervision provides a safe reflective learning space for wise conversation.

I identify the critical reflection process and the dialogical sharing process mentioned above as containing some key elements for supervisory practice in a postmodern culture. I will now explore further the underlying and operative theory of "wise supervision," that is, wise collaborative conversation leading to transformational learning, a process that can help learner and supervisee reach authentic wisdom or sagehood.

Wise Collaborative Conversation

Writers such as Robert Kegan, Lisa Lahey,[11] and Margaret Wheatley,[12] when writing about organizational change, alert us to the importance of changing our conversation. Conversations create, reveal, sustain, or change organizational culture, uncovering what is acceptable or unacceptable. Our intentions drive our conversations. Often conversation is understood as a tool for getting what we want or for convincing another of our point of view. Conservation reveals what we see in the world and the meaning we attach to what we see. Engaging in new conversation, what I call wise collaborative conversation, is one of the most effective ways to create ongoing and lasting transformation in our practice, organizations, and in society.

Wise collaborative conversation is rooted in a rich wisdom tradition in spirituality and a more recent growing understanding of the concept within psychology. The study of wisdom has a history that long antedates psychological study, with the Platonic dialogues offering the earliest record of a sustained analysis of the concept of wisdom.[13]

Within these dialogues there are three different aspects of wisdom. There is wisdom as *sophia*, found in those who seek a contemplative life in search of truth; *phronesis*, the "practical wisdom" of statesmen and legislators; and *episteme*, a form of scientific knowledge. Teachers of wisdom in the Judeo-Christian Tradition engage in wise conversation that discerns what gives life and what does not. For Sophia, the personification of Wisdom in the Scriptures, the goal of teaching is rich life and transformation for individuals and communities.

Two types of wisdom are evident in the Scriptures, conventional and subversive wisdom. Conventional wisdom, concerning the laws and principles of the dominant power or culture, is less relevant to our conversation than the subversive wisdom of the New Testament Scriptures. This radical wisdom offers in invitational mode a wisdom perspective on the depths of reality. It is an invitation to a new perspective and a new way of being in the reality of the present that may lead to transformation. It is an invitation to contemplatively listen and be attentive to the cries of wisdom, as she dwells in both the human heart and the world. This is a universal wisdom that is also evident in the contemplative path and mindfulness of the Buddhist tradition. It is a subversive wisdom that follows the energy of what is life giving.

The concept of *wisdom*, as rooted in positive psychology—a new branch of psychology primarily concerned with the scientific study of human strengths such as resilience and resourcefulness—captures the essence of the generative nature of the supervisory space and an effective cross-professional supervisor.

Drawing on psychological and spiritual aspects of wisdom, we see that wisdom is considerably more than knowledge and is developed over time (see Figure 4).

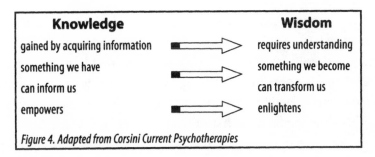

Figure 4. Adapted from Corsini Current Psychotherapies

Within Sternberg's[14] balance theory of wisdom, wisdom involves applying tacit knowledge to problem solving in a way that achieves a balance among three interests—intrapersonal, interpersonal, and extra personal—and three possible responses to this balancing, that is, adapting or shaping oneself or others to existing environments or selecting new environments. Practical wisdom balances one's own interests and those of others involved with the problem with the wider community to achieve a common good for all.

Building on this theory, supervision as wise collaborative conversation spirals inwards and outwards, moving through four levels simultaneously in search of wisdom, the common good for all. In wise conversation there is a constant balancing of gathering information (*content*), holding interiority contemplatively (*intrapersonal*), tending to right relationship (*interpersonal*) and witnessing to the mystery of emerging wisdom (*extrapersonal*).

Using the four levels of wise collaborative conversation as a lens to reflect on Kevin's dilemma, a lens which I use within supervisory practice, Kevin seeks out the common good through a balancing of his own interests (*intrapersonal*) with the interests of his clients, trainees and the profession (*interpersonal*), and a new world of meaning that is emerging as he experiences this deep shift in vision with a transformative potential for himself, others, and society (*extrapersonal*). In this context, Kevin wisely chooses a balance between adaptation and shaping—which requires flexibility—as he is open to changing himself and playing his part in also changing the environment. As Kevin selected the objects and created his garden, the process was simultaneously moving between the content, intrapersonal and interpersonal levels, with glimpses of the extrapersonal emerging too. I, as supervisor and reflective witness, cultivated an attitude of attentive receptivity, leading to understanding and openness to the emerging wisdom.

As any experienced gardener knows, a garden cannot be mastered or controlled. Gardening is about drawing out the resources of nature by allowing each element to contrast with, highlight, and balance one another. It is about identifying what is already there, balancing, adapting, and selecting the existing element rather than creating it. The role of the gardener is that of balance keeper, to learn from nature and to seek a natural order. The heart of gardening is finding the correct balance. Attention to the levels of wise conversation supports establishing equilibrium.

Collaborative Learning

Supervision has evolved from its historical meaning of overseeing the supervisee to a more collaborative process between supervisor and supervisee. Supervisors act as facilitators of collaborative learning who support and challenge supervisees' strengths, limitations and resources, and provide a safe learning environment in which the supervisee is helped to take responsibility for their own learning and practice. Critical reflection on personal practice needs to be undertaken alongside open discussions and reflective discourse with others as the assumptions and premises that guide our ways of constructing knowledge are assessed and, whenever necessary, revised.

Wise conversation is not just a spoken dialogue; it involves a listening to the wisdom of the heart, to the voice of wisdom in others and in the world. Mezirow points to the importance of critical friends:

> Any critically reflective effort we undertake can only be accomplished with the help of critical friends. We need others to serve as critical mirrors who highlight our assumptions for us and reflect them back to us in unfamiliar, surprising and disturbing ways. We also need our critical friends to provide emotional sustenance.[15]

A truly collaborative venture is both potentially exciting and potentially uncomfortable. Collaborative learning means learning as a social and collaborative process. Although uncomfortable for some academics, the creation of the learning group, and the importance of relationships with others in fostering transformative learning, has proven to be an indispensable aspect of the MA program in cross-professional supervision. As participants discover their voices and their inner wisdom, they are invited to move beyond technical rationality— that is, beyond being passive receivers of knowledge and skill—towards becoming constructors of knowledge. Within a collaborative learning group, participants develop the art of conversation and skill in giving and receiving feedback. For this they need a well-developed sense of self and assertiveness. Everyone is part of the learning community and every contributor is respected. Knowledge is negotiated and meaning is co-constructed.

Many supervisors and supervisees seem to be in search of the one right answer. Such a search rests in a view of intelligence that emphasizes outcomes and expert authority. Effective supervisors ask questions. A collaborative approach moves away from debate and the familiar hierarchical expert-novice relationship and a top-down learning process. Instead, collaborative learning promotes a receptive, non-judgmental environment that is supportive of critical self-reflection on assumptions. The challenge for supervisors within this approach is to resist the urge to provide information, answers and immediate action as they cultivate the skill of purposeful reflective questioning, using such tools as Bloom's revised taxonomy.[16]

The systematic use of questions cultivates a sense of wonder and encourages curiosity within the learning relationship. Good supervisors learn to refine the questions rather than search for the right answers, thus balancing their desire to be "wise" with their desire to be "right." Waiting with the questions requires an inner security, an inner wisdom, and a capacity to live with paradox and unknowing which has been described by Keats as "negative capability."[17] Uncertainty creates the freedom to discover meaning as we free ourselves from preconceived ideas we unknowingly carry and become aware that there are other equally valid, alternative perspectives. Wise collaborative supervision is a form of conversation with self and others, a conversation in which the exploration of meaning is more important than being "right." Respecting the inner wisdom of the supervisee, the supervisory process is concerned with calling forth a wise person rather than seeking the "right" answer.

Adopting a Meta Stance

Wise collaborative conversation also involves developing the ability to take a meta perspective, that is, the ability to monitor one's current state of learning, a key skill in the supervisory process. Bolton describes reflection in action as "the hawk in your mind constantly circling over your head watching and advising on your actions—while you are practicing."[18] Effective supervisors help supervisees to develop the capacity to take a meta stance, that is to set aside prejudgments, biases, and preconceived ideas about things. This unfettered stance or wise, egoless way of seeing challenges the supervisee to adopt a fresh way of looking and being. Kevin demonstrated a well-developed capacity for reflection in action, as he symbolically took a meta stance by sitting on the rock to reflect on the landscape of his professional journey and practice (see Figure 5). The symbolic use of objects in wisdom's garden for supervision has a distancing effect that may create safety for the supervisee to explore difficult or challenging issues. Cognizant of the boundaries between supervision and therapy, the role of the supervisor is to facilitate learning by engaging the supervisee's "internal supervisor" and his/her capacity for wise collaborative reflection.

Figure 5

To embody distancing and the perspective of a meta stance, Kevin stood up to look down on his garden. It was only with this change in perspective that he noticed the large lotus flower between himself and the two figures (see Figure 5). He was surprised how he had filtered the lotus flower out of his awareness as it was the largest symbol in the garden. He had no conscious memory of choosing it. As he reflected on this experience, he realized that it in some way expressed how he had learned to filter out the contemplative, spiritual dimension in himself professionally, despite its prominence. He felt it was the "something more" that he was seeking and found that it was already present. As he moved among the four levels of wise collaborative conversation, he saw the two seated figures in the garden from a new perspective.

A garden is a fenced plot of ground, enclosed and bounded on a horizontal but not on a vertical plane, and so when Kevin stood up, he experienced this meta position in an embodied way. This helped him to visually take a meta stance so that he might gain a more objective, creative view of his situation, opening up the possibility of new insight and perspective. When reviewing the session, Kevin shared how he had gained deep insight at this moment. Following this experience he decided to engage in spiritual guidance, a space where he could explore and develop this aspect of his identity more deeply. Thus wise collaborative conversation may lead to action. Within the supervisory process we also renegotiated the contract to include the reflective, spiritual aspect in our work together in a way that was both appropriate and respectful of boundaries. Supervisors need to wisely and creatively stake the boundaries of the supervisory process to ensure that they meet the learning needs of the supervisee. During the process of wisdom's garden, Kevin was invited to change or re-create his garden by removing or adding something, or by removing himself from the garden. This phase of the process helps to underscore any insight, learning, or wisdom gained that may be brought back into practice, thus completing the action-reflection-action cycle.

Conclusion

As I embrace the emerging future and continue to develop my understanding of supervision, the use of wisdom's garden within one-to-one and group supervision has led me to think differently about the supervisory process, and most importantly, how meanings are constructed through wise collaborative conversation that support supervisees' ability to survive and prosper in challenging environments. My internal supervisor has been strengthened and I am reminded that outstanding practitioners do not have more professional knowledge than others but more skill, talent, artistry and wisdom.[19]

Being a supervisor today is an exciting and challenging responsibility. At its best, the art of supervision provides a safe holding environment which facilitates wise collaborative conversation that can lead to trans-formation. Wisdom stands at the crossroads, the place of wise conversation, the interface of many disciplines such as philosophy, sociology, theology, psychology, political science, spirituality and literature. Hildegard of Bingen, the twelfth-century German mystic, in one of her songs, *The Antiphon to Wisdom*, describes wisdom as having three wings. One points to the earth, the place where wisdom stands at the crossroads. This may be understood as pointing to the pertinent situation or experience. A second points to the heavens, perhaps pointing to a new perspective, meta stance, or subversive perspective. The third moves freely between the two in the holding environment between the human heart and the world, gathering insight and learning from the wise collaborative conversation that can lead to transformation and wisdom.

It is my hope that as supervisors stand, individually and collectively, at the crossroads of change, they will continue to be open to transformation through critical reflection and collaborative conversation and to finding creative ways to hear wisdom's voice in individuals, organizations, and society, so that the future of the profession can be more accountable, ethical, and ultimately more effective and wise. The soul of supervision for me involves seeking balance and tending to this wisdom task. I conclude by recalling the wise words of Martin Buber:

> There is meaning in what for long was meaningless. Everything depends on the inner change; when this has taken place, then and only then, does the world change.[20]

Notes

[1] J. E. Loder, *The Transforming Moment* (Colorado Springs: Helmers and Howard, 1989), 2.

[2] M. Carroll, *Counselling Supervision: Theory, Skills and Practice* (London: Cassell Publishers, 1996).

[3] P. Berger and T. Luckman, *The Social Construction of Reality: A Treatise in the Sociology of Knowledge* (London: Penguin Books, 1996).

[4] J. Mezirow and E. Taylor, *Transformative Learning in Practice: Insights from Community, Workplace, and Higher Education* (San Francisco: Jossey-Bass, 2009).

[5] J. Mezirow, "The Critical Theory of Adult Learning and Education." *Adult Education*, 32, 3–24.

[6]J. Mezirow, *Transformative Dimensions of Adult Learning* (San Francisco: Jossey-Bass, 1991).

[7]J. M. Bernard and R. K. Goodyear, *Fundamentals of Clinical Supervision* (Upper Saddle River, NJ: Pearson, 2009).

[8]ANSE stands for the Association of National Supervisors of Europe.

[9]S. D. Brookfield, *Developing Critical Thinkers: Challenging Adults to Explore Alternative Ways of Thinking and Acting* (San Francisco: Jossey-Bass, 1987).

[10]T. Hart, "From Information to Transformation: Education for the Evolution of Consciousness," *Counterpoints: Studies in the Post Modern Theories of Education Volume* (Vol. 162).

[11]R. Ryan and L. Lahey, *How the Way We Talk Can Change the Way We Work: Seven Languages of Transformation* (San Francisco: Jossey-Bass, 2001).

[12]M. Wheatley, *Turning to One Another: Simple Conversations to Restore Hope to the Future* (San Francisco: Berrett-Koehler Publishers, 2007).

[13]Daniel Robinson in R.J. Sternberg, ed., *Wisdom: Its Nature, Origins, and Development* (Cambridge: Cambridge University Press,1990), 13–24.

[14]R. J. Sternberg, *Wisdom, Intelligence and Creativity Synthesized* (Cambridge: Cambridge University Press, 2003).

[15]J. Mezirow, "The Critical Theory of Adult Learning and Education," *Adult Education*, 32:3–24.

[16]B. S. Bloom, *Taxonomy of Educational Objectives* (Boston: Allyn and Bacon, 1984).

[17]W. J. Bate, *Negative Capability: The Intuitive Approach in Keats* (New York: AMS Press, 1976).

[18]G. Bolton, *Reflective Practice-Writing and Professional Development* (London: Paul Chapman Publishing, 2001)

[19]D. Schon, *The Reflective Practitioner* (New York: Basic Books, 1983).

[20]M. Buber, *Good and Evil* (New York: Scribner's Sons, 1953), 5.

Bibliography

Bate, W. J. *Negative Capability: The Intuitive Approach in Keats.* New York: AMS Press, 1976.

Bakan, D. *On Method: Toward a Reconstruction of Psychological Investigation.* San Francisco: Jossey-Bass, 1969.

Belenky, M. F., B. M. Clinchy, N. R. Goldenberger, and J. M. Tarule, eds. *Women's Ways of Knowing: The Development of Self, Voice and Mind.* New York: Basic Books, 1997.

Benefiel, M. *The Soul of a Leader.* New York: Crossroad Publishing Company, 2008.

Berger, P. and T. Luckman. *The Social Construction of Reality: A Treatise in the Sociology of Knowledge.* London: Penguin Books, 1966.

Bernard, J. M. and R. K. Goodyear. *Fundamentals of Clinical Supervision*. Upper Saddle River, NJ: Pearson, 2009.

Bloom, B. S. *Taxonomy of Educational Objectives*. Boston: Allyn and Bacon, 1984.

Bolton, G. *Reflective Practice: Writing and Professional Development*. London: Paul Chapman Publishing, 2001.

Brookfield, S. D. *Developing Critical Thinkers: Challenging Adults to Explore Alternative Ways of Thinking and Acting*. San Francisco: Jossey-Bass, 1987.

Buber, M. *Good and Evil*. New York: Scribner's Sons, 1953.

Corsini, J. R. and D.Wedding, eds. *Current Psychotherapies*. Eighth Edition. Belmont, CA: Thomson Books/Cole, 2008.

Carr, A. *Positive Psychology: The Science of Happiness and Human Strengths*. Sussex and New York: Routledge, 2004.

Carroll, M. *Counselling Supervision: Theory, Skills and Practice*. London: Cassell Publishers, 1996.

Carroll, M. and M.Tholstrup, eds. *Integrative Approaches to Supervision*. London and Philadelphia: Jessica Kingsley Publishers, 2001.

Casement, P. *Learning from the Patient*. London: Travistock, 1985.

Conroy, M. *Looking into the Well: Supervision of Spiritual Directors*. Chicago: Loyola Press, 1995.

Cranton, P. *Professional Development as Transformative Learning; New Perspectives for Teachers of Adults*. San Francisco: Jossey-Bass, 1994.

Friedman, H. S. and R. R. Mitchell, eds. *Supervision of Sandplay Therapy*. Hove, NY: Routledge, 2008.

Hall, S. *Wisdom: From Philosophy to Neuroscience*. New York: Alfred A. Knopf, 2010.

Hart, T. "From Information to Transformation: Education for the Evolution of Consciousness." *Counterpoints: Studies in the Post Modern Theories of Education Volume*, vol. 162.

Hawkins, P. and N. Smith. *Coaching, Mentoring and Organizational Consultancy: Supervision and Development*. Berkshire, UK: Open University Press, 2006.

Kegan, R. and L. Lahey. *How the Way We Talk Can Change the Way We Work: Seven Languages for Transformation*. San Francisco: Jossey-Bass, 2001.

Langer, E. J. *Counter Clockwise: Mindful Health and the Power of Possibility*. New York: Ballantine Books, 2009.

Loder, J. E. *The Transforming Moment*. Colorado Springs: Helmers and Howard, 1989.

Merton, T. *The Inner Experience: Notes on Contemplation*. London: SPCK, 2003.

Mezirow, J. "The Critical Theory of Adult Learning and Education." *Adult Education*, 32 (1981): 3–24.

Mezirow, J. *Transformative Dimensions of Adult Learning*. San Francisco: Jossey-Bass, 1991.

Mezirow, J. and E. Taylor. *Transformative Learning in Practice: Insights from Community, Workplace, and Higher Education*. San Francisco: Jossey-Bass, 2009.

Mishler, E. G. *Research Interviewing: Context and Narrative*. Harvard: Harvard University Press, 1991.

Rohr, R. *The Naked Now: Learning to See as the Mystics See*. New York: Crossroad, 2009.

Scaife, J. *Supervision in the Mental Health Professions: A Practitioner's Guide*. Hove, NY: Brunner-Routledge, 2001.

Schön, D. *The Reflective Practitioner*. New York: Basic Books, 1983.

Shohet, R. J. *Passionate Supervision*. London and Philadelphia: Jessica Kingsley Publishers, 2008.

Sternberg, R. J., ed. *Wisdom: Its Nature, Origins, and Development*. Cambridge: Cambridge University Press, 1990.

Sternberg, R. J. *Wisdom, Intelligence and Creativity Synthesized*. Cambridge: Cambridge University Press, 2003.

Ward, F. *Lifelong Learning: Theological Education and Supervision*. London: SCM Canterbury Press, 2005.

Wheatley, M. *Turning to One Another: Simple Conversations to Restore Hope to the Future*. San Francisco: Berrett-Koehler Publishers, 2007.

Chapter

2

∾

The Transformative Power of Journaling:

Reflective Practice as Self-Supervision

ഌ *David McCormack* ഗ

I n my workplace (an adult education center), I facilitate groups that focus on personal growth and development and that promote transformative learning. In one such group, I experienced a particularly negative atmosphere: a number of people appeared unmotivated and a number seemed to be quite distressed as a result of our explorations. I felt constantly criticized and undermined. I blamed myself, feeling that more experience, or better training, or a less reserved personality would have saved the group from failure.[1]

A Hurry Through Which Known and Strange Things Pass

Seamus Heaney has written of what I will call a transformational moment, that is, a moment when daily life and consciousness is surprised into awareness in a way that transforms perspective. In the poem "Postscript," he describes a scene of unusual beauty and dynamism in County Clare, a scene that heightens the poet's awareness of his own preoccupied mood. Having evoked the beauty and dynamic power of the scene he says:

> Useless to think you'll park and capture it
> More thoroughly. You are neither here nor there,
> A hurry through which known and strange things pass
> As big soft buffetings come at the car sideways
> And catch the heart off guard and blow it open.
>
> (Heaney, 1996: 444)

Such a moment can be used as a reference point for people in caring professions. Our lives can be without a doubt "a hurry through which known and strange things pass," while much of the time our jobs require us to have a vigilant heart that is very much on guard. Like the poet, the caring listener needs to be at once on duty and off guard, available as a listening presence and, at the same time, available to the surprise of self and other.

Professional carers include those in ministry, pastoral care, counselling, spiritual direction, and education: in other words, any profession where the goal is to contribute positively to another's growth and development. Since the self is the core instrument in caring professions (Wosket, 2004), there is a clear need for that self to be listened to and cared for in supportive and challenging ways. The standard way of doing this is in supervision.

I have come to rely on my supervision as a way to maintain myself in my work and to heighten my awareness of myself as a practitioner. At the same time, this self-awareness is an ongoing process that needs to be kept alive at all times in daily practice. Accordingly I have also come to rely on journal writing as an approach to professional development and this has prompted me to research further into journaling as a form of reflective practice and self-supervision (Hawkins and Shohet, 2000: 5–30). This chapter will review key literature concerning journaling as an approach to reflective practice leading to transformative learning, in the context of the critical incident from my own experience summarized above.

Transformative Learning

Mezirow's formulation of transformative learning theory is often taken as the classic version. For Mezirow, people have a "meaning perspective" consisting of the frames of reference they have about the world. These perspectives are derived from the socialization process but are vulnerable to our own adult experience of the world. Any disturbance to them can cause a dilemma which leads to self-examination and which ultimately can lead to perspective transformation:

> Perspective transformation is the process of becoming aware of how and why our assumptions have come to constrain the way we perceive, understand, and feel about our world; changing these structures of habitual expectation to make possible a more inclusive, discriminating, and integrating perspective; and finally, making choices or otherwise acting upon these new understandings. (Mezirow, 1991:167)

Baumgartner (2001) demonstrates how this strand of transformational theory is currently being expanded. Firstly, the transformational learning journey is no longer viewed as a linear process, but as a "complex process involving thoughts and feelings." Secondly, the disorienting dilemma is no longer viewed solely as a single dramatic event, but the theory allows for the possibility of it being a "long cumulative process." Thirdly, the importance of relationships in the transformational learning process and the role of context and culture are being recognized and acknowledged (Baumgartner, 2001: 18).

In a more recent restatement of his theory, Mezirow (2000) offers the following as hallmarks of perspective transformation:
> A disorienting dilemma
> Self-examination with feelings of fear, anger, guilt, or shame
> A critical assessment of assumptions
> Recognition that one's discontent and the process of transformation are shared
> Exploration of options for new roles, relationships, and actions
> Planning a new course of action
> Acquiring knowledge and skills for implementing one's plans
> Provisional trying of new roles
> Building competence and self-confidence in new roles and relationships
> A reintegration into one's life on the basis of conditions dictated by one's new perspective

(Mezirow, 2000: 22)

Journaling

There is considerable evidence that journal writing can be a creative and dynamic way of maintaining vibrant contact with one's inner life in a way that can lead to personal development (Hunt and Sampson, 1998), professional development (Bolton, 2001), and depth learning (Moon, 2003).

Journaling, as Dyment and O'Connell assert, is "an enduring human practice" (2000: 2). It is increasingly recommended both in learning settings" (Moon, 2003) and as a tool of professional development and reflection (Moon, 1999). According to Moon, journal writing enhances the writer's capacity for metacognition, which is "the understanding of a person about her own mental processes" (2003: 4). It encourages reflection and this is "associated with deep approaches to learning," that is, the kind of learning where "the intention of the learner is to develop a personal understanding of the material" (2003: 4). Moon views journaling as a process that accentuates favourable conditions for learning that "produces intellectual space in which we can think" and that "encourages independent learning" (2003: 4).

Journaling is one way of using writing as a mode of inquiry (Richardson, 1997; Richardson and St Pierre, 2005) into professional and personal experience. As an approach to reflective practice (Bolton, 2005, 2006, 2010), writing can "be a deeply questioning enquiry into professionals' actions, thoughts, feelings, beliefs, values, and identity" (Bolton, 2006: 203–4). Writing as an approach to reflective practice allows us to make our taken-for-granted world strange (Bolton, 2006: 204), transmuting experience into a created object available to dialogue. Such an approach offers "the illuminative power of explorative and expressive writing to develop understanding" (Bolton, 2006: 216).

For Bolton, too, reflective writing is an opportunity to put our thoughts and feelings into writing in order to reflect, share, and develop the issues raised. For her there is a paradox at work in the notion of writing as reflective practice. In order to acquire confidence as an effective practitioner one needs to let go of certainty.

> *The confident, effective practitioner is the one who is able to respond flexibly and creatively to a range of influences, needs and wants of clients or colleagues, and unforeseen events and forces. A practitioner who thinks they know the right answers all the time is bound to be wrong. (Bolton, 2001: 33)*

The focus in Bolton's approach to professional reflection is always on our thoughts, feelings, and actions (Bolton, 2001, 15), but more specifically she recommends that we should focus on areas of vulnerability so that we work at our "cutting edge" (Bolton, 2001: 159). She says that "the writing process . . . is creative, a way of gaining access to each practitioner's deep well of experience not always accessible to everyday channels" (Bolton, 1999: 195).

> *Writing is used because it is essentially different from talking. It can enable the writer to make contact with thoughts and ideas they did not know they had, with completely forgotten memories, and enable the making of leaps of understanding and connections. It can also enable the expression and exploration of issues which the writer is aware of, but unable or unwilling otherwise to articulate, communicate and develop. (Bolton, 1999: 195)*

Reflective writing in journal form is an increasingly widespread way of allowing people to connect with the narrative aspect of their experiences (Rossiter, 2002). Ricoeur has established such an understanding as a constructive way of viewing the self and the development of the self over time. A narrative view allows us to "integrate into one whole and complete story multiple and scattered events, thereby schematising the intelligible signification attached to the narrative as a whole" (Ricoeur, 1984: x). The implication of this version of identity is that "the person, understood as a character in a story, is not an entity distinct from his or her experiences. Quite the opposite: the person shares the condition of dynamic identity peculiar to the story recounted" (Ricouer, 1992: 147). Ricouer concludes then "it is the identity of the story that makes the identity of the character" (Ricouer, 1992: 148). It follows that telling such stories of our selves in journal form enhances our understanding of the self, both the self of the practitioner and the self of those with whom we work.

D. Best reflects on her use of a learning journal as a professional worker during an advanced training course. She views journaling as "one way of guiding and charting the process of exploration and of reaching insights to inform learning and practice" (Best, 1998: 153). Writing for her became a way of integrating the three areas of her life as a professional, a learner, and an individual self with "a personal world of self, family, and others" (Best, 1998: 153). She claims "integrating those spheres through writing and reflecting on the learning process has led me to understand the creative potential of writing as a keenly appropriate tool for training" (Best, 1998: 153).

Journaling in her view entails "regular and committed writing to record thoughts and feelings about every aspect of work and development, leading to a reflective piece to review progress and identify emerging themes" (Best, 1998: 154). It is also a way of managing and processing feelings, particularly feelings of distress and disturbance.

Two poles of reaction to such distress are possible, to implode or to explode. In other words I may take the experience into myself and not find ways of processing it, or alternatively I may blurt it out, or dump it on someone, again without thinking it through, feeling the feelings, and so on. This is where the journal can provide a holding space that can help us to feel what we need to feel, to think through incidents and events in a way that is healthier for ourselves and for others (Best, 1998: 156–7). Containment is therefore an important aspect of journaling whereby "putting words on paper fixes a version of reality, but at the same time makes it available for reconsideration. Sometimes the very process of writing may prompt subtle shifts in perspective; then re-reading—receiving back the material—allows the thoughts and feelings to return in modified form, making it more possible to reconsider them" (Best, 1998: 157).

Journaling then as an activity that is conducive to processing professional experiences, particularly experiences that are disorienting or distressing, is an important resource in professional life. Through our journals we are in a position to process intrapersonal and interpersonal relationship issues, much as we do in supervision, but in a way that is more accessible and frequent.

Journaling about a Critical Incident

Josephs (2008) talks of "resonant moments" and the part they play in emergent learning. McCormack (2009) suggests that such moments may be used as autoethnographic explorations of professional practice. In the critical incident summarized at the beginning of this chapter, my journal became an anchor point that I used before and after each group. Free floating with ideas, using many of the techniques proposed by Bolton (2001), often using poetry, story making, and retelling stories from different points of view, I most often used the journal as a place to express the heightened feelings I had about this group.

On one particular occasion I was free writing in my journal (Murray, 2005: 74) and a particular image arose, apparently from nowhere, of a snake shedding its skin. I wrote, as always, without questioning what came up. The following day the group began, as usual, with complaints and a combination of people not taking the group seriously and others dealing with their acute distress by blaming. But something changed that day and I had no idea why. The distress began to be heard by others and a dialogue ensued in which I had no part other than as a time and boundary keeper. The depth of contact between the group members was extremely touching. There was real contact at a deep level I had never encountered before with this group that involved mutuality, care, and concern for each other. Towards the end of the group I asked, as I often did, for a word from each group member. The round started and each group member shared, very touchingly, his or her authentic reactions to the process. The last person to speak had said very little throughout the group and I wondered what she would say. She very simply said, "I'm sitting here with an image of a snake shedding its skin."

I was stunned. I had been taking complete responsibility for the apparent "failure" of the group. No matter how many times I processed the issues in supervision, I remained deflated and dejected and feeling incompetent. The coincidence of the two images, however, enabled me to reconnect with the power of relationship. This was, in fact, a matrix of relationship that had its own dynamic, albeit a predominantly distressing one, and that dynamic had culminated in a transformative experience.

Anxiety and Transformative Learning

The process of learning in adult life is "an intrinsically emotional business" (Claxton, 1999: 15) and so it was for both me and the group in this story. The story embodies the process of working in the powerful emotional context in which much of adult learning occurs (Dirkx, 2001, 2006) and points up the way in which the emotional dimension of working with adults operates at subtle levels of our selves. Dirkx (2006: 22) draws attention to how the unconscious aspects of learning about ourselves can surface in images as well as in behaviors, as it did when the snake entered my journal.

The story about my experiences working with an otherwise recalcitrant group places anxiety at the heart of the educative experience. West (2006) offers us a view of how lifelong learning takes place in the context of a postmodern condition. Anxiety stems from a sense of discontinuity and fracture where grand narratives of "familial templates or uncontested knowledge" (West, 2006: 41) are no longer available. This anxiety is generally hidden but will be expressed in a variety of ways.

> Anxiety, especially around threats to the self, can generate a whole range of defensive manoeuvres, often unconscious . . . in adult learning. These manoeuvres focus themselves around, for instance, our capacities to cope, or whether we are good enough, or are acceptable to, or even deserve to be accepted by, others. (West, 2006: 42)

The story suggests the need to rehabilitate rather than disown anxiety and points up the possibilities for growth and change. Coping with anxiety requires the appreciation of the educative arena as a "transitional space" where "identity may be negotiated and risks taken in relation to potentially new identities" (West, 2006: 42).

Narratives operate at a level not immediately amenable to conceptualization. Initially I understood my experiences in terms of a narrative of personal inadequacy. However, the denouement I experienced subsequently was of a more revelatory, transpersonal story that could be understood in terms of unconscious processes. In this version of the story, issues of transference and counter-transference, understood as unconscious processes in myself as practitioner and in the group, were being played out and gradually loosened up and resolved in the matrix of the group. The story's center of gravity was not on any one of the selves in the story; no one narrative was privileged in the experiencing, though it is in the re-telling. Instead the denouement was an expression of something that co-emerged from a shared space (Fenwick and Tennant, 2004). It did not emerge from any intentionality on the facilitator's part. Indeed the transformation was what happened when the intention to transform had long ago been abandoned in favour of survival, and therefore some aspects of paradox are at work in the story.

Heaney's poem, "The Riddle," has been helpful to me in understanding the pattern of experience that emerged in working with the group. In the poem Heaney uses the image of a riddle, understood at one level as a sieve for grain or sand, and at another level as a puzzling question, to sift through questions relevant to anyone whose intention is to "do good." The poem surfaces fundamentally puzzling questions about values, about what is good or bad in human choices. It enacts the process of sifting grain and asks what is more valued, that which falls through or that which is retained. There is also a sifting at a more psychological level of questions of value, power, and agency in the image "of the man who carried water in a riddle/Was it culpable ignorance, or was it rather/ A *via negative* through drops and let downs?" (Heaney, 1987: 51).

The poem suggests to me that the intention to set out to "do good," though in itself a central element of ethical practice, is not a guarantee either of success or of good practice. Indeed there may be more value in the mistakes and disappointments of our work than in the unproblematic use of our skills.

The pattern of experience in the critical incident was one of puzzling distress leading to unexpected and unhoped-for insight. It is best understood as a *via negative*, rather than as the planned execution of a set of skills and competencies. It was an experience whose meaning for me and for the group only emerged over a long time and that required a huge amount of sifting in supervision and in my journaling to process it and stay alive to its potential for learning and transformation.

Conclusion

The complexity of any caring endeavor in the postmodern world is self-evident and the demand on the carer is huge. Hawkins and Shohet view supervision as of crucial importance in the caring professions. They maintain "supervision can be a very important part of taking care of oneself and staying open to new learning, as well as an indispensable part of the helper's ongoing self-development" (Hawkins and Shohet, 2000: 5). They say:

> We have found that when we have been able to accept
> our own vulnerability and not defend against it, it has

been a valuable experience both for us and our clients. The realization that they could be healing us, as much as the other way around, has been very important both in their relationship with us and their growth. It is another reminder that we are servants of the process. (Hawkins and Shohet, 2000: 15)

My experience has been that self-supervision in the form of journaling is as important for my own professional development and reflective practice as has been my formal supervision. It has allowed me to contain and to work creatively with my own vulnerability and has provided me with a medium where I can accept, work with, and value my own vulnerability as a crucial resource in the work. When I can support myself to accept my vulnerability and to remain at my own growing edge, I increase the chances of holding, supporting, and challenging others at their growing edges. In my experience that acceptance and vulnerability has invariably been a gateway to the kind of growth that emerges from the shared space of dialogue. In this way the revelatory power of the caring relationship can be held in a creative form.

Note

[1]Though this took place in my own professional life, I have altered important details to protect the identity of the people involved.

Bibliography

Baumgartner, L. M. 2001. "An Update on Transformational Learning," *New Directions for Adult and Continuing Education*, 89, (Spring).

Best, D. 1998. "On the Experience of keeping a reflective journal while training." In *Intuition is not Enough: Matching Learning with Practice in Therapeutic Child Care*, Ward, A. and McMahon, L. London: Routledge.

Bolton, G. 1999. "Reflections through the looking-glass: The story of a course of writing as a reflexive practitioner." *Teaching in Higher Education*, 4(3): 193–203.

Bolton, G. 2001. *Reflective Practice: Writing and Professional Development*. London: Chapman.

Bolton, G. 2006. "Narrative writing: Reflective enquiry into professional practice." *Educational Action Research*, 14(2):203–18.

Bolton, G. 2010. *Reflective Practice: Writing and Professional Development*, 3rd ed. London, Sage.

Boud, D. et al. 1993. *Using Experience for Learning*. New York: Oxford University Press.

Boud, D. 2001. "Using Journal Writing to Enhance Reflective Practice." *New Directions for Adult and Continuing Education*, 90(Summer):9–17.

Brookfield, S. 1995. *Becoming a Critically Reflective Teacher*. San Francisco: Jossey-Bass.

Claxton, G. and Atkinson, T., eds. 2003. *The Intuitive Practitioner*. Buckingham: Open University Press.

Claxton, G. 1999. *Wise Up: The Challenge of Lifelong Learning*. London: Bloomsbury.

Dirkx, J. M. 2001. "The Power of Feelings: Emotion, Imagination, and the Construction of Meaning in Adult Learning," *New Directions for Adult and Continuing Education*, (Spring), 63–72.

Dirkx, J. M. 2006. "Engaging Emotions in Adult Learning," *New Directions in Adult and Continuing Education*, (109), 15–26.

Dyment, J. and O'Connell, T. 2003. "Journal Writing in Experiential Education: Possibilities, Problems, and Recommendations." ERIC Digest ED479358, www.eric.ed.gov. Accessed 8/09/05.

Fenwick, T. and Tennant, M. 2004. "Understanding Adult Learners." In *Dimensions of Adult Learning: Adult Education and Training in a Global Era*, ed., G. Foley, ed. Maidenhead: Open University Press.

Gardner, H. 1993. *Multiple Intelligences, The Theory in Practice: A Reader*. New York: Basic Books.

Gilbert, M. and Evans, K. 2000. *Psychotherapy Supervision: An Integrative Relational Approach to Psychotherapy Supervision*. Buckingham: Open University Press.

Hawkins, P and Shohet, R. 2000. *Supervision in the Helping Professions*, 2nd ed. Berkshire: Open University.

Heaney, S. 1996. *Opened Ground: Poems 1966–1996*. London: Faber and Faber.

Heaney, S. 1987. *The Haw Lantern*. London: Faber.

Hunt, C. and Sampson, F. 1998. *The Self on the Page: Theory and Practice of Creative Writing in Personal Development*. London: Jessica Kingsley.

Inskipp, F. and Proctor B. 1993. *The Art, Craft and Tasks of Counselling Supervision*. Twickenham, UK: Cascade.

Josephs, C. 2008. "The Way of the S/Word: Storytelling as Emerging Liminal." *International Journal of Qualitative Studies in Education*, 21(3):251–267.

McCormack, D. 2009. "A Parcel of Knowledge: An Autoethnographic Exploration of the Emotional Dimension of Teaching and Learning in Adult Education." *The Adult Learner: The Irish Journal of Adult and Community Education*. Dublin: Aontas: 13–28.

McLeod, J. 2003. *An Introduction to Counselling*, 3rd ed. Buckingham: Open University Press.

Mezirow, J. 1991. *Transformative Dimensions of Adult Learning*. San Francisco: Jossey-Bass.

Mezirow, J. 2000. "Learning to Think Like an Adult." In *Learning as Transformation: Critical Perspectives on a Theory in Progress*, Mezirow, J. and Associates. San-Fransisco: Jossey-Bass.

Miller, N. and Boud, D. 1996. *Working with Experience: Animating Learning*. London: Rouledge.

Moon, J.A. 1999. *Reflection in Learning and Professional Development: Theory and Practice*. London: Kogan-Page.

Moon, J. 2003. "Learning Journals, Their Use Across the Disciplines and a Review of Assessment Issues." Paper delievered at University College Dublin, CD, May 2003.

Murray, R. 2005. *Writing for Academic Journals*. Berkshire: Open University Press.

Ricoeur, P. 1992. *Oneself as Another*, trans. K. Blainey. Chicago and London: University of Chicago Press.

Ricoeur, P. 1984. *Time and Narrative*, Vol. 1, trans K. McLaughlin and D. Pellauer. Chicago and London: University of Chicago Press.

Rossiter, M. 2002. "Narrative and Stories in Adult Teaching and Learning." ERIC Digest, ED473147, www.eric.ed.gov. Accessed 8/09/05.

Scaife, J. 2001. *Supervision in the Mental Health Professions: A Practitioner's Guide*. Hove: Brunner-Routledge.

Schön, D. 2002. "From Technical Rationality to Reflection-in-Action." In *Supporting Lifelong Learning: Volume 1, Perspectives on Learning*. London: Routledge Falmer.

Tudor, K. and Worrall, M. 2004. *Freedom to Practise: Person-Centred Approaches to Supervision*. Ross-on-Wye: PCCS Books.

Vaill, P. 1996. *Learning as a Way of Being: Strategies for Survival in Permanent White Water*. San Francisco: Jossey-Bass.

Walker, D. 1985. "Writing and Reflection." In *Reflection: Turning Experience into Learning*, eds. D. Boud, R. Keogh and D. Walker. Sydney: Kogan Page.

Wosket, V. 2004. "The Unfolding of the Therapist's Use of Self." *Eisteach*, 3(1):12–16.

Chapter

3

~

Nurturing Ministerial Leadership Through Supervision

~ Debora Jackson ~

R ev. Sheila Morgan was wrapping up some closing details in her office after worship one Sunday morning, when an urgent rap at the door interrupted her thoughts. "May I come in?" Tom asked. Tom Roberts was the church's student minister and Sheila served as his supervisor. Noticing his intensity, Sheila rose to welcome Tom into her office and closed the door behind him. Something was coming; she just wasn't sure what it was.

"What's up?" Sheila asked, trying to keep her tone light.

"I want to talk about today's worship service," Tom said. "What I really want to talk about is the sermon," he quickly added.

One of Tom's internship goals was to preach on a regular basis. He had preached the morning worship service. The sermon went fine, but there were distractions. Specifically, Blair and Sarah Johnson's six-month-old daughter, Julia, cried from the moment the sermon started until its conclusion. That had to be the issue. Sheila found herself bracing for Tom's response.

"We need to do something about babies crying in the worship," Tom blasted. "My sermon was absolutely ruined. Do you think that anyone was able to hear what I had to say? No! They were too distracted by a crying baby."

Sheila started to interject, but Tom kept speaking.

"Parents need to be told that if their children are crying, they need to leave the sanctuary," Tom stated point blank. "In fact, I think we need to put that statement in the bulletin and specifically speak to the Johnsons so that they will not allow this to happen again."

As human beings, we make meaning of our situations and we do it in an instant.[1] What is the process by which we make meaning? The first thing that we do in making meaning is to unconsciously filter the data of our surroundings, testing it against pre-established expectations. Particularly as adults, we organize information relationally, associating concepts with beliefs, culture, values, and norms that are influenced by our environment. This relational model of data is like a schematic—

a blueprint that serves to help us quickly relate any new data to our existing mental model. New data is compared, instantaneously and unconsciously, to our schematic map. Thus, we draw meaning from that comparison. From a positive perspective, this is an effective way of reaching conclusions about the situations that confront us. On the other hand, there is an inherent shortcoming in this data-filtering stage. If the new data that we receive does not fit our schematic map, it is often disregarded as extraneous. Therefore, only data that reinforces our schematic model is retained, serving to reinforce our convictions about the conclusions that we draw as we make meaning.

As an example, consider how you have already summarized the situation with Sheila, Tom, and the Johnsons regarding their crying baby. What should Sheila do? What would you do? Certainly the literature on pastoral supervision has much to say that would shape the conversation between supervisor and supervisee. In fact, such conversations provide a primary basis of pastoral supervision.

According to Kenneth Pohly, "Pastoral supervision is a method of doing and reflecting on ministry in which a supervisor and one or more supervisees covenant together to reflect critically on their ministry as a way growing in self-awareness, ministering competence, theological understanding, and Christian commitment."[2] As a pastoral supervisor, Sheila has the responsibility, in covenant relationship, to work with Tom to reflect on ministry activities in ways that will increase his awareness of his ministerial role and competence, while also deepening his understanding of his faith tradition and commitment to it. This work of reflection is connected to that of meaning making. Through reflection, we are effectively invited to examine how things look and what they mean from a new vantage point.[3] But for what purposes do we engage in such reflection? Experts in the field would suggest that there are at least four growth-oriented purposes for pastoral supervision: to help people understand themselves more clearly; to assist in the development and refinement of ministering competencies; to sharpen and clarify theological understanding; and to deepen Christian commitment.[4] Yet, these purposes seem to miss one critical component.

Given our own personal reactions to the situation with Sheila, Tom, and the Johnsons, we recognize the need to come to "the right conclusions," but how do we, as pastoral supervisors, foster an environment in which we can come to such conclusions? We do it through leadership. Leadership is the work of seeing that the right things are done, versus the work of management, which is concerned about doing things the right way.[5] This is a critical but underemphasized role in pastoral supervision. We have a vital responsibility to nurture leadership in those we supervise so that in their practice of ministry, our supervisees are better prepared to ensure that the right things are done. Certainly there are numerous competencies that are suggested as necessary to aid in this work of leadership.[6] However, as a starting point, pastoral supervisors can help to nurture leadership in those we supervise through a process of reflection that enables them to make meaning and determine courses of action faithfully and in broader, more expansive ways.

Scott Cormode suggests that this is our first duty as Christian leaders: define reality by providing a Christian perspective for those under our leadership.[7] By doing so, pastoral supervisors provide an interpretative framework for meaning making, through which theological categories consisting of names, interpretations, and commitments are developed to describe a situation.[8] The result of such leadership is that people are enabled to make meaning for themselves, paving the way for faithful action. It follows then that we nurture leadership in those we supervise by helping them to make meaning of a situation through a process of defining reality. As pastoral supervisors this means that we provide a theological framework by which meaning is made and faithful action is initiated.

Taking a deep breath, Sheila says to Tom, "If I understand you correctly, you are upset because Julia Johnson cried through your entire sermon, and you felt that her crying distracted both you and the congregation. Is that correct?"

"Yes," Tom replied, still reacting to the situation.

"You were also upset because you felt that the Johnsons should have recognized that the crying was distracting and that they should have left the sanctuary with the baby, right?" Sheila added.

"Absolutely," said Tom. "I can't imagine why they didn't just get up and leave. It's not like we don't have a nursery that they could have gone to."

"Yes, I hear you," Sheila said. "But before we launch into what could have or should have been done, let's just pause a minute. Are there any parallels from scripture or our faith tradition that fit this situation?"

"I don't know, but I certainly don't remember Jesus having to put up with crying babies during his sermons," Tom quipped sarcastically.

"No?" said Sheila. "I do. Do you remember the story where parents were trying to bring their children to Jesus to be blessed and the disciples were pushing them away and speaking to the parents harshly?"

"Yes," Tom said sort of sheepishly. "Jesus said, 'Suffer the children to come unto me.'"

As pastoral supervisors, we have the wealth of biblical resources at our disposal to help in constructing the theological framework that can broaden the meaning-making process. The scriptures become important ways to help us expand our thinking. Because we ascribe the authority of our religious beliefs to scripture, scriptures have the power to provoke our thoughts, persuade, and reorient our modes of meaning making.

Consider Jesus as he delivered the Sermon on the Mount. The religious leaders of Jesus' day had a defined standard of righteousness that fell far short of the standards demanded by Jesus. Notwithstanding, those standards projected by the religious leaders dictated the norms that defined acceptable behavior. To disturb that model, Jesus needed to demonstrate that what was generally recognized as acceptable was insufficient. He had to provoke new thoughts, use provocation to persuade and then change thinking in order to reorient the way that his listeners made meaning. In a series of "You've heard it said . . . , but I say to you . . ." statements, Jesus compared and contrasted acceptable behavior to righteous behavior. In doing so, he provoked doubt in what was thought to be acceptable. This cognitive dissonance that he inspired created receptivity to a new way of thinking as people tried to rationalize the discrepancy in their practices and his teaching. Prefacing that new way with the phrase, "But I say to you," he persuaded his listeners to recognize that they had fallen far short of the glory of God. For those who received his words, the conversation initiated a conversion experience whereby people came to faith in God through Jesus Christ.

Pastoral supervisors have these same means at their disposal. We need to leverage the power of scriptures to do exactly what Jesus did.

We use the scriptures to provoke thoughtfulness, causing our supervisees to reflect on a situation and elicit a new response. Then we use the scriptures to persuade our supervisees to consider a new mental model. Creating cognitive dissonance between a held belief and a new way of thinking, supervisors nurture leadership by increasing the potential for a transformative moment for the supervisee.

Tom paused and thought. "Is that your way of saying that I should have been more tolerant and patient with the Johnsons and not gotten upset that the baby was crying?"

"Well, I'm not sure that it's as simple as that," Sheila responded. "But what do you think? I understand that you were annoyed, but what do you do with that?"

"You know, I don't know," Tom said. "I was annoyed. Sure, I want children to be in the worship service, but in that moment, when I was trying to preach and couldn't hear myself think, I really didn't want that kid in the sanctuary. The sermon is too important not to be heard."

"Hmm," said Sheila, "You said that you want children to be in the worship service but at the same time you said that you don't want crying children in the worship service." Sheila allowed the silence to permeate the room.

Tom stared blankly at Sheila before responding. "I guess that makes me sound sort of neurotic."

"No," Sheila quickly interjected. "This is not about passing judgment. I'm just sharing with you what I heard you say."

"Yeah, but the two expectations are in conflict or are at least unfair. How can I say that I only want children who can be quiet in worship?" Tom asked.

"It's not an unheard of expectation, Tom," Sheila offered. "Churches have long held an expectation that kids would be quiet and behaved in worship. Even in society, the old adage was that children should be seen and not heard."

"But that expectation sounds like the dark ages. How do we sound when we say that children should be seen and not heard?" replied Tom.

"Isn't that what you were demanding when you came in?" Sheila asked, smiling.

"Yeah, I suppose so," Tom chuckled.

This is an important revelation and one that cannot be overlooked as we seek to nurture leadership in those we supervise. Doubt occurs for Tom as he is confronted by the cognitive dissonance that exists between what he says he believes versus what his actions confirm as his beliefs. Tom says that he believes that children should be in the worship, but is angry when a child's presence disrupts the worship. Had Tom been asked before the situation whether he believed that children should be part of a worship service, he probably would have said yes. However, given the situation of a child crying during the worship, he no longer was in favor of this particular child's presence.

This is a key observation. How someone will behave in a certain situation cannot be determined by asking the person.[9] People will honestly believe that they will behave in one manner, but their actual behavior may be different. What people believe their behavior will be is called espoused theory, whereas how people actually behave in the moment is called lived theory.[10] Dissonance exists when a gap occurs between our espoused theory and lived theory.[11] In response, we will either reconcile the dissonance in order to attain consistency between our beliefs and our actions or we will discount what is dissonant in order to trivialize the conflict between what we espouse and how we live. This latter reaction impairs our meaning-making abilities and causes meaning-derived conclusions to be narrowed and myopic.

Dissonance between our beliefs and our actions can also happen theologically. Tom believed that children should be welcomed in worship, just as Jesus welcomed the children that the disciples tried to discourage from coming. However, his belief encountered dissonance when a child was not able to behave in a way that was in alignment with the expectations of Tom's lived theory. An unstated expectation was that the child would be silent during the sermon. Moreover, if the child was unable to remain silent, then the parents would intercede and remove the child from the sanctuary. The unstated expectation for Tom was a legitimized standard.[12] His lived theory, supported by his mental model, deemed a specific behavior as appropriate. In other words, people are expected to be silent during the sermon. When the child was unable to be silent and the parents opted not to remove the child to maintain silence, Tom's legitimized standard was violated, thus exposing the gap between Tom's espoused theology and his lived theology. His lived theology demanded that the sermonic moment be held as sacred and without distractions.

As Tom's pastoral supervisor, Sheila had the opportunity and responsibility to help uncover the discrepancy between what Tom espoused and what he lived. By helping Tom to see how what he said he believed differed from his actions, Sheila was positioned to nurture leadership by expanding Tom's ability to make sense of a situation with greater openness and receptivity. The challenge for us as supervisors, however, is to do this in a way that will allow the supervisee to be nurtured in the learning. By maintaining a supportive environment while helping our supervisees consider a situation from an objective perspective, we nurture leadership by lowering the barriers of defensiveness, encouraging non-threatening reflection, and helping the supervisees envision their role in the situation.

Chapter 12 of 2 Samuel provides a wonderful example of this. In this narrative, God sends the prophet Nathan to King David. Prior to this narrative, David went to great lengths to conceal his covetousness of Bathsheba, the wife of Uriah. Yet being so possessed by his desire for Bathsheba, David refused to acknowledge his own wrongdoing. Nathan had the responsibility of helping David see the error of his ways. Nathan maintained a supportive environment by using a story-telling narrative. He tells David a story of a rich man who had great wealth as evidenced by his numerous flocks and herds. This man was contrasted to a poor man who had nothing but a single lamb. Nathan continued his story by describing how the rich man took the lamb from the poor man, leaving him with nothing. David, upon hearing the story, became angry and immediately declared to Nathan that the rich man should die. Having helped David recognize the injustice of the situation, Nathan was then able to say to David, "The man is you."

Pastoral supervisors provide this same type of leadership for supervisees. As the narrative about Tom's experience demonstrates, individual judgment and perspective can be clouded at times, given our own subjectively and close proximity to a situation. Moreover, being too close to a situation causes us to become defensive when challenged. Thus, pastoral supervisors nurture leadership in those they supervise by helping them to consider their behaviors in new and less subjective ways that will break down the defenses that block learning.[13] Without such means, people become defensive when asked to critically reflect upon their own role in a situation. Rather than gain benefit from the reflection, the more common reaction is to place blame, projecting it onto others and rarely onto self.

Thus, supervisors nurture leadership by broadening the view, enabling supervisees to be more objective in the process of making meaning. Chiefly through a capacity to deeply reflect on a situation, supervisors help supervisees seek information that may lead them to enhance, refine, or alter their perspectives to be more inclusive of new ideas.[14] We must encourage our supervisees to pause, to reflect in the moment, and to consider through the traditions of our faith the conclusions that they make. In this way, we are more able to objectively view a situation and become more expansive in our meaning-making process.

This broadening of our meaning-making ability is a chief skill, particularly considering the relationship between meaning making and establishing a course of action. As quickly as we make meaning of a situation, drawing upon our schematic map that is composed of culture, ideas, and values, we also make a determination about a course of action. The limitation of this process, however, is that there is a deterministic aspect to the actions that we conceive. We will view them as right and legitimate given our meaning-making process. Therefore it becomes as important for us as supervisors to help those under our leadership expand the range of possible actions that result from having made meaning so that the actions considered offer the broadest perspective.

One of the primary goals of Christian ministry is "faithful action."[15] Faithful action is action that is proven and upheld by the traditions of the faith, efficacious in its ability to adaptively address the needs and concerns of the community, and undergirded by spiritual disciplines that foundationally support and rationalize the actions to be taken.

How do the traditions of our faith help us to faithfully act? First, we must understand the traditions and how God speaks through those traditions. This calls for us, as pastoral supervisors, and for those we lead, to know and be able to gain understanding from interpreting the word of God to truly understand God. However, this is only a starting point because it is not enough for us to simply understand. The word of God calls us to action. As the prophet Micah notes in Micah 6:8, "Oh mortal, what is good; and what does the Lord require of you but to do justice, and to love kindness and to walk humbly with your God?" Faithful action requires that we understand and then use that understanding to motivate action that is consistent with God's leading.

For example, in the narrative of Jesus welcoming children, the disciples were motivated to act. However they failed to test their actions through the lens of faith as taught by Jesus. Believing that the children were perhaps too young to benefit from the effect of the blessing or too bothersome to come before Jesus, they thought it important to discourage parents and prevent them from bringing their children to Jesus. This action was consistent with the meaning that they made, and as a result the disciples thought it an appropriate action to discourage parents from bringing the children to Jesus for blessing.

However, the disciples' meaning making and resultant action was inconsistent with Jesus' teachings. Jesus taught that the Kingdom of heaven belongs to those who are like children: open, ready, and willingly receptive. Given the meaning of this teaching, the resultant action should have been to not only welcome children, but also emulate them in our practices. We nurture leadership as pastoral supervisors by helping supervisees test the validity of actions through the lens of faith. In doing so, we encourage faithful action that is consistent with and motivated by the traditions of our faith.

Faithful action is also efficacious in that it adaptively addresses the needs and concerns of the community. Consider the communal needs and concerns that leaders face. Many of the answers to those needs are elusive. Having never seen the combination of variables and complexities that comprise the various challenges that we face, we as leaders simply do not have all of the answers to the problems. This fact is the distinguishing characteristic between technical challenges and adaptive challenges. Technical challenges are those for which we "know" what needs to be done. In contrast, adaptive challenges are those problems for which the know-how does not yet exist.[16] Recognizing that we as leaders do not have all of the answers, it then becomes necessary for us to engage others in the process of problem solving. In nurturing leadership, pastoral supervisors are called to show supervisees how to mobilize people so that together the community is prepared to face the tough realities and conflicts that are encompassed in communal challenges.[17] Supervisees must recognize that they will not have all of the answers to the difficult challenges that face their congregations. Therefore, they must learn to work in ways that galvanize and motivate the entire community to act. Not only does this effort create buy in for those involved, but it also brings the best ideas to the fore. So, our role as pastoral supervisors is to encourage reflection that considers the inclusion of key constituents that will help the community faithfully respond to the challenges that confront it. In this way, the ownership of the work is shared and the actions are distributed.

"Seriously, Tom, if you felt this strongly that this was a problem, I'm sure others did too."

Tom asked, "Maybe there are some people who want to come together to talk about this. Do you think that we could have a brainstorming session?"

"Sure. Is there anyone in particular that you'd want to see us invite?" Sheila asked.

"Maybe the ushers could be a part of a conversation. They might be the ones asked to do something if this happened again. We could also invite some of the mothers and fathers. Certainly, they would have ideas about what would be most helpful," said Tom.

Sheila added, "Great idea! I would also think that some of the deacons should be present as well, since they are responsible for the membership. Whatever conversation we have, we should try to make it a community effort."

Thus faithful action looks to engage the broader community in order to identify adaptive ways to solve issues. Additionally, faithful action is undergirded by spiritual disciplines that foundationally support and rationalize the actions to be taken. Spiritual disciplines are like a training regimen that is freely incorporated into one's life for personal benefit.[18] In this instance, the personal benefit is the growth and development of one's spiritual life. As this benefit is applied to supervision, the benefits are extended to both the supervisor and the supervisee.

What makes spiritual disciplines effective for leadership is that their application provides an intentional means by which we encounter the divine and become more receptive to God's leading. Spiritual disciplines give us the space and grace to nurture an inner life so that we might step back and assess a situation with a non-anxious spirit. In addition, the intentionality that results from our practices informs our decision making and helps us to identify the best solutions.

There are a number of disciplines that we can readily incorporate in our faith lives. Reflection is a primary practice for leadership. "The source of real learning in one's leadership is within oneself, and each one must train him- or herself in the new skills needed to be a reflective person."[19] Other practices include spiritual reading methods such as *Lectio Divina*, through which we can reflect on the word and allow it to permeate our beings. The practice of prayer and gathering for worship can be life giving. The daily examen process of considering that for which we are most thankful, versus that for which we are less thankful, is a powerful centering exercise.[20]

Specific disciplines notwithstanding, our efforts with those we supervise can begin as modestly as helping our supervisees to consider where God is in the midst of a situation and how God might be speaking to them in the moment. The purpose of our practices is to help supervisees go deeper into God. As they do this, they gain clarity and focus for the actions that they consider.

"Ok, so we convene this gathering. How do we shape the meeting so that everyone is held and supported in the conversation?" Sheila asked.

"Well," said Tom, "this is definitely a time when we need to extend hospitality."

"Hospitality?" responded Sheila. "Say more."

"When you think about it, it was obvious that Blair and Sarah were having some troubles with Julia because she was crying through the service. But no one extended themselves to help. By the same token, for the people who were annoyed by the crying, don't we also need to extend hospitality to them by offering a worship experience without unnecessary distractions?"

"Yes, we do. We need to extend hospitality to the entire congregation," Sheila nodded thoughtfully. "So how could we have extended hospitality in that moment?"

"Well, maybe an usher could have gone to the Johnsons and invited them to take Julia to the nursery," said Tom in response.

"Yes," said Sheila, "that would have been a possibility. What else? Specifically, what could you have done?"

"Well," thought Tom. "Maybe I could have said something to the congregation. Maybe I could have said something like, 'It's all right, babies cry sometimes.'"

"Or," Tom suggested brightly, "maybe I could have gone and picked up Julia myself or at least walked over to the Johnsons as a show of support."

Another strategy that pastoral supervisors can use to nurture leadership is action reflection. In this "thinking-on-our-feet" model, action-reflection involves looking to our experiences, connecting with our feelings, and in real time, building new understandings to inform our actions in the situation as it is unfolding.[21] Tom's brainstorming of different ways to respond to the baby's crying were good examples of this kind of action-reflection. In doing this, however, the challenge becomes one of remaining open to multiple understandings and interpretations in order to prevent premature adoption of any one action.[22] As pastoral supervisors, we can encourage action-reflection through what-if questions that stretch thinking, while also providing a net of support that serves to undergird the process.

"All of these are great possibilities and certainly considerations if this ever happens again," said Sheila. "Going forward from today, what do you think that we should do?"

"Well, it seems like there are a few conversations needed," said Tom.

Sheila nodded her assent and by doing so encouraged Tom to continue.

"I think I would like to convene a group of folks to talk about how we can more hospitably extend ourselves to young families. I think we need to do something about babies crying during worship, but we can't react in ways that will alienate families with children."

"I agree. That makes sense," said Sheila.

"I guess I also want to talk to the Johnsons, but I know that it will be a different conversation than I wanted to have when I first came in," offered Tom.

"How so?" asked Sheila.

"I think I have to follow the example of Jesus and be more welcoming of children," Tom said. "I thought that I was welcoming, but maybe not.

I think I also need to extend hospitality. And in that spirit, I guess I want to ask the Johnsons if there is anything that we can provide by way of assistance should Julia start crying in church."

"Good. Anything else?" asked Sheila.

"Yes. I guess I need to say thank you, Pastor Sheila. You listened and helped me through this. I feel a lot better now."

"I'm glad to have been here for you, Tom," said Sheila. "Would you like to close in prayer . . . ?"

So much of what we do as pastoral supervisors is to help train and prepare those who are under our leadership for ministry. Certainly we ready them to do tasks—preaching, teaching, visitations, and the like. These are important skills to have in one's ministerial toolkit. However, the greatest challenges for pastors do not lie in performing the basic tasks of ministry. We know how to do that. The real work lies in preparing pastors for the kind of leadership that will propel the church forward and foster an adaptable and flexible readiness that is able to respond to a diversity of challenges.

This chapter has contended that pastoral supervisors can begin this work by nurturing leadership in the practice of supervision. A key strategy identified in this process was in helping supervisees make meaning of situations through the lens of faith and from the broadest perspectives. Related was the strategy of faithful action, which similarly opens the options of possible actions that can be considered, once one has made meaning of a situation. However, the underlying and unifying thread through this chapter has been the process of nurturing—the work that is done by pastoral supervisors. In our work with supervisees, pastoral supervisors stretch, challenge, and provide space for our supervisees to engage in thoughtful consideration. We also provide the support that makes it possible for the safe exploration of such considerations. And it is through such nurture that we help to shape and prepare those under our leadership to become meaning-making, faithfully acting leaders themselves.

Notes

[1]Robert Kegan, *The Evolving Self: Problem and Process in Human Development* (Cambridge: Harvard University Press, Cambridge, 1982), 11.

[2]Kenneth Pohly, *Transforming the Rough Places: The Ministry of Supervision* (Franklin, TN: Providence House Publishers, 2nd ed., 2001), 107–8.

[3]Robert L Kinast, *Let Ministry Teach: A Guide to Theological Reflection* (Collegeville, MN: The Liturgical Press, 1996), 130.

[4]Pohly, *Transforming the Rough Places*, 108.

[5]Norman Shawchuck and Roger Heuser, *Leading the Congregation: Caring for Yourself While Serving the People* (Nashville, TN: Abington Press, 1993), 20–21.

[6]Daniel Goleman, Richard Boyatzis, and Annie McKee, *Primal Leadership: Realizing the Power of Emotional Intelligence* (Boston: Harvard Business School Press, 2002). Specific competencies include Self-Awareness (emotional self-awareness, accurate self-assessment, self-confidence); Self-Management (self-control, transparency, adaptability, achievement, initiative, optimism); Social Awareness (empathy, organizational awareness, service); Relationship Management (inspiration, influence, developing others, change catalyst, conflict management, teamwork and collaboration).

[7]Scott Cormode, *Making Spiritual Sense: Christian Leaders as Spiritual Interpreters* (Nashville, TN: Abington Press, 2006), xi.

[8]Ibid., 12–13.

[9]Chris Argyris and Donald A Schön, *Theory in Practice: Increasing Professional Effectiveness* (San Francisco: Jossey-Bass, 1974), 7.

[10]Ibid., 30.

[11]Argyris and Schön, *Theory in Practice*, 31.

[12]Cormode, *Making Spiritual Sense*, 41.

[13]Chris Argyris, *Teaching Smart People How to Learn* (Cambridge: HBR OnPoint, Harvard Business School Publishing Corporation, 2000), 6.

[14]Robert Kegan and Lisa Laskow Lahey, *Immunity to Change: How to Overcome It and Unlock the Potential in Yourself and Your Organization* (Boston: Harvard Business Press, 2009), 21.

[15]Scott Cormode, "Constructing Faithful Action: Inculcating a Method for Reflective Ministry," *Journal of Religious Leadership*, Vol. 3, No. 1 and No. 2, Spring 2004 and Fall 2004, 228.

[16]Ronald A. Heifetz, *Leadership without Easy Answers* (Boston: Harvard University Press, 1994), 72.

[17]Ibid., 21.

[18]Marjorie J. Thompson, *Soul Feast: An Invitation to the Christian Spiritual Life* (Louisville, KY: Westminster John Knox Press, 2005), 10.

[19]Leonard Doohan, *Spiritual Leadership: The Quest for Integrity* (New York: Paulist Press, 2009), 74.

[20]Dennis Linn, Sheila Fabricant, and Matthew Linn, *Sleeping with Bread: Holding What Gives You Life* (New York: Paulist Press, 1995), 6.

[21]Donald A. Schön, *Educating the Reflective Practitioner* (San Francisco: Jossey-Bass, 1987), 28.

[22]Ronald A Heifetz, Alexander Grashow, and Marty Linsky, *The Practice of Adaptive Leadership: Tools and Tactics for Changing Your Organization and the World* (Boston: Harvard Business Press, 2009), 120.

CHAPTER

4

∾

Learning on the Road:

Pastoral Supervision as a
Form of Ongoing Formation

೫ *Martin McAlindin* ೬

A lex is a hardworking and effective pastor of a large urban parish in Northern Ireland. Despite the collaboration with an active pastoral council and a number of parishioners who are involved in ministry, he finds it burdensome at times to engage in the normal, day-to-day pastoral activities expected of him. When he meets with his colleagues, the conversation inevitably turns to the lack of morale that exists among clergy. Alex is aware that no other profession is being criticized so severely these days and that criticism is eroding his priestly identity and confidence. He feels disillusioned with priesthood and is frustrated at the lack of support being offered to clergy from those in leadership and their lack of vision for the future. He is concerned about the declining number of priests in active ministry. "How will I cope in the future when there are fewer priests and I am older?" is a question that often worries Alex.

Alex's story is not uncommon. In Ireland at least, self-confidence is low and disillusionment is high among Catholic priests, which can make it difficult for them to muster enthusiasm and freshness for ministry. As they observe trained lay people taking up pastoral positions which were once the preserve of the clergy, they can feel threatened and lacking in professional skills. There is a growing realization among priests that ministry is no longer simply the vocation of the ordained or religious; it is also a profession that demands best practice.[1]

In coming years issues relating to morale and identity will continue to loom large not just for clergy, but also for laity as they negotiate their role in ministry. Priests like Alex, as well as lay pastoral workers, will need support as they work together to build up God's Kingdom. Pastoral supervision can offer an important form of professional care and ongoing formation.[2]

This chapter, written from my experience as a supervisee and supervising clergyperson, offers a tool box of models, theories, and resources that may be useful to supervisors interested in working with pastoral ministers. It sees pastoral supervision as an integrative and contemplative process which is sensitive to the transitions happening in the church and ministry, transitions which impact the life of clergy and lay workers alike. The story of how the disciples when walking along the road to Emmaus processed the death of Jesus is used to illustrate this process.

Defining Pastoral Supervision

In Luke 24:13–35 two disciples are walking to Emmaus on the evening of the resurrection "talking together about all that had happened" (Luke 24:14). Jesus joins them, and as he walks by their side asks them "what are you discussing with each other as you walk along?" (Luke 24:17). In telling their story of disappointment and despair they reveal a lack of understanding about the full identity and mission of Jesus, and consequently a lack of understanding about their own identity and mission. John Shea notes, "They have all the facts and none of the meaning."[3] Meaning-making (or revelation, or transformation) happens for them when Jesus helps them make sense of the facts, in this case by revealing himself by explaining the Scriptures to them and breaking the bread. We are told that the disciples return instantly to Jerusalem and begin to proclaim the resurrection (Luke 24: 33–34).

This gospel scene is a simple example of pastoral supervision at work: the disciples are encouraged to tell the story of what is happening in their lives; with Jesus they reflect on the facts; and they return to where they came from with new meaning and enthusiasm. The story suggests that an integrative and contemplative model of pastoral supervision has at least three distinct aspects: it offers a broad space to talk about whatever is happening in ministry; it is sensitive to God's voice and to the spiritual; and it effects transition and transformation, often subtly, resulting in the minister returning to the place of ministry with enhanced "self-awareness, ministering competence, theological understanding, and Christian commitment."[4]

The Broadness of Ministerial Experience

They were talking together about what had happened.
—Luke 24:14

In most professions the material presented in supervision is often specific, focusing on work with clients, supervisor and supervisee issues, and organizational matters. Pastoral ministry is different. The church has traditionally described three functions of ordained ministry, namely preaching, shepherding, and celebrating divine worship.[5] These tasks point to a great variety of ministerial experiences that can be brought to supervision, whether the supervisee is an ordained minister or professional lay person. For instance, a priest may wish to review his preaching style, the theological content of his homilies, or his commitment to preparing sermons. Similarly, a minister might seek help with shepherding by reviewing pastoral planning, discussing her relationship with other clergy, parishioners, or the pastoral council, reflecting on how she exercises power and authority, evaluating her ability to delegate, and talking about ethical dilemmas or experiences of stress and burnout. Under the category of divine worship come equally diverse possibilities: the evaluation of a particular funeral liturgy, reflection on how one approaches a preparation talk for First Holy Communion, or an exploration of the tensions experienced when celebrating the sacraments with those who no longer go to church.

While supervision offers a space to reflect on the wide variety of experiences and relationships in pastoral work, there is more to ministry than work. Ministry is a vocation and so the life and work of a minister are inseparable. Alex is an effective priest, but his work is becoming burdensome for him, not because he lacks ability but because he is disillusioned with priesthood and anxious about the future. In supervision, this experience of disenchantment and his fears need to be heard and held. At the heart of an integrative reflection on ministry, space needs to be given for clergy and laity to talk about their lives, their dreams and hopes, their vision of ministry, and what ministry is doing to them. In supervision Alex might profitably spend time reflecting on the support systems he has in his life and exploring with his supervisor a vision for ministry in a time when there is a shortage of priests.

The ability to help supervisees deal with the broad experiences of ministry and the effects of ministry on their lives can be aided by access to a wide range of resources. In addition to understanding integrative and process models of supervision, I have found the following books useful for pastoral supervision.

> ❭ *The Heart and Soul of Parish Ministry* by Regina Coll reflects on the meaning of ministry.

> ❭ *Lifelong Learning: Theological Education and Supervision* by Frances Ward explores the nature of ministry and formation for the twenty-first-century church.

> ❭ *Helping the Helpers: Supervision and Pastoral Care* by John Foskett and David Lyall uses Ekstein and Wallerstein's "clinical rhombus" to describe the sometimes complex tension that ministers experience as representatives of the institutional church and at the same time pastors.[6]

> ❭ *Pastoral Supervision: A Handbook*, edited by Jane Leach and Michael Patterson, offers a practical guide to the supervision of pastoral work.[7]

> ❭ *Rest in the Storm* by Kirk Byron Jones aids supervisees in reflection on self-care.[8]

Practical resources from unexpected quarters, for example "after action reviews" developed by the U.S. Army,[9] might also be incorporated into supervisory work when helping ministers talk about all that is happening.

Sensitivity to God's Voice and Guidance

Jesus himself came up and walked by their side.
—Luke 24:15

Christian ministry is primarily a response to a personal invitation of Christ to get to know him. The order is clear in John 21:15–17—Jesus asks Peter three times "Do you love me?" It is only when Peter answers "yes" that he is called to ministry. In my own experience, I can get so bogged down in "work" that I forget to nurture my relationship with the God who calls me to ministry. I am convinced that pastoral supervision needs to facilitate an encounter between those in ministry and the source of their faith. It is this relationship which helps them make sense of the bits and pieces of their lives and which gives ultimate meaning to their ministry.

The supervisor can honor the presence of the One who walked with the disciples on the road by asking explicit questions about God and faith such as: "What is God saying to you now about this experience? Where was God when you spent time with that bereaved woman? In what ways has this tragedy affected your image of God? What was life-giving about your ministry since our last session? Which biblical texts resonate with your experience?" Alex, for instance, might gain valuable insight and renewed vision for priesthood by reflecting on Jesus' experiences of disenchantment in the gospels. He might be encouraged to talk about the spiritual disciplines that are nurturing his life at present. Such spiritual questions allow supervisees to "think deeply and vulnerably about life and values, work and career, relationships and connections"[10] so that their life and work rhyme. Pastoral theologians call this integration "theological reflection" and offer models particularly useful for supervision.

For Jim and Evelyn Whitehead, theological reflection is "the process of bringing to bear in the practical decisions of ministry the resources of Christian faith."[11] Three sources of information, namely the Christian tradition, personal experience, and cultural resources,[12] are brought into dialogue in a three-stage method of attending by 1) seeking out the information from these three sources on a particular pastoral concern and listening to it uncritically; 2) bringing the information into a lively dialogue; and 3) developing a pastoral response.[13] This is really what occurred in Luke's Emmaus story: meaning-making happened as the experience of the two disciples, their socio-political hopes, Scripture, and the breaking of the bread were brought into dialogue. The pastoral response was an enthusiastic return to Jerusalem to proclaim the resurrection.

This model could be profitably used with Alex, as well as with those charged with pastoral planning in his diocese, to create a vision of ministry less dependent on ordained ministers. His own story of ministering in a time of scarcity and the experience that exists among the lay people who minister in his parish could be brought into dialogue with the Tradition (e.g., Vatican II definitions of ministry, diocesan pastoral letters, the Scriptures) as well as with cultural and social concerns, including statistics about declining numbers of clergy and the importance of self-care. In reflecting theologically about low morale, a more spiritual, reflective focus which promotes a thick description of Alex's experience of priesthood might be useful. Patricia O'Connell Killen suggests the importance of attending to inner dimensions when describing experience (e.g., feelings, thoughts, attitudes, and hopes that Alex carries into ministry) and outer dimensions (e.g., the people, places, projects, and objects that surround him and with which he interacts).[14] I have discovered that this deep focus on experience is also useful in reflecting on day-to-day pastoral experiences that are brought to supervision.

In her book *Looking into the Well*, Maureen Conroy describes a contemplative model of supervision for spiritual directors which encourages, like spiritual models of theological reflection, an inner focus on experience.[15] A pastoral supervisor, working with Alex and adopting Conroy's model, would focus on the importance of nurturing a contemplative presence, i.e., fostering an evocative or exploratory process which allows him to stay with his inner experiences in an open-ended way so that he develops a discerning heart.[16] Such a supervisor would also explicitly acknowledge the sacred space that supervision is. In my own work I begin each session with a few moments of silence in order to bring to awareness the presence of God in the supervisory relationship.

Conroy's model of supervision can look like spiritual direction, perhaps even counseling. However, supervisees only process personal issues that affect their ministry and in doing so grow in self-awareness and ministerial competence. Knowing when to refer supervisees for spiritual direction or therapy is an important skill supervisors need to possess.

Ministers such as Alex need to feel safe in order to share personal issues and experiences of ministry. Successful supervision requires good supervisory relationships. Kenneth Pohly, instead of talking about supervisory contracts, talks about "covenant." This scriptural word, with its connotations of God's faithful, unconditional commitment to God's people, might be useful in assuring ministers that the supervisory relationship is one of faithfulness, commitment, and trust. Trust only develops with time, and will be helped if the relationship is one of mutuality. In this regard, I have discovered that appropriate sharing of my own experiences of vulnerability and failure in ministry can help nurture mutuality and give supervisees permission to be honest and vulnerable.

In working with Alex, it might be helpful if a priest-supervisor shared his vision of priesthood and the type of support systems he has in his life.

Transition and Transformation

Our own hope had been.

—Luke 24:21

Luke 24:21 records the words of two disillusioned and grieving disciples. Their hopes have been dashed. As they walk away from Jerusalem their identities are shattered. The Jesus they had followed is dead, and they do not know who they are anymore. Symbolically, darkness falls. Jesus challenges them to stay with the story and in doing so the light of meaning begins to shine. Ironically, what happened in the city gives them their future identity. The narrative ends with them travelling back to Jerusalem with renewed energy, wisdom, and enthusiasm. A transformation has occurred. The movement for these disciples is from ending, through a period of reflective uncertainty, to new beginning. This is the pathway of transition.[17]

In many ways pastoral supervision, in staying with the story of what is happening in ministry, facilitates subtle transformation, as supervisees gain new insight and return to parishes or chaplaincy work with renewed passion. At times it also helps ministers negotiate important transitions. In that regard, the process of pastoral supervision can be helpful to Alex as he reflects deeply on his disillusionment and dashed hopes. It can provide a secure and caring space to stay with painful experiences and feelings he has instead of running away. An understanding of the psychological dynamics of transition can help in the formation of clergy and other pastoral workers, helping them discover that in endings and dashed hopes are new beginnings. Such work will impact on their vision for ministry and their relationship with God.

With Alex, and with others trying to make sense of change in supervision, the first task is to name what is ending. For the disciples on the road it is their belief that Jesus would be an ethnocentric messiah. For contemporary clergy in ministry, including myself, so much seems to be ending—vocations to ordained ministry and religious life, the church's moral authority, and models and theologies of ministry and church that sustained clergy in the past but which no longer seem to fit. The identity question "Who am I now?" is all too familiar.

To acknowledge that endings are happening is to be launched into loss and grief. Zullo notes, "loss disrupts our ability to find meaning; grief represents our struggle to retrieve meaning."[18] As a minister I have discovered that supervision offers a valuable supportive space to grieve as I come to terms with the reality of child sexual abuse and disillusionment with church and priesthood. It asks what structures and coping strategies I have in place to enable me to live and cope with uncertainty and endings. It also facilitates the exploration of assumptions, beliefs, styles, and models of ministry.

The work of grief moves a person into an in-between time in transition, described helpfully by Marion Woodman as "the twilight zone between past and future that is the precarious world of transformation."[19] Part of the grief for Alex is because long-held assumptions and beliefs about ministry and priesthood are beginning to lose their power in his life, and he is confronted with nothing to put in their place. This is the time of struggling to re-vision ministry, priesthood, and models of church; as well, it is a rich opportunity for pastoral supervision to facilitate the movement into new beginning. However, this movement needs to be at the supervisee's pace; in my own experience, talking about the future grates if it doesn't fully honor the present.

The movement into a new beginning, or transformation, is a spiritual awakening. The Emmaus story tells us that it is a holy encounter that leads to life. Pastoral supervision can facilitate the successful navigation of transition while assuring ministers that crisis and change are normal, to be embraced rather than feared.

Supervisors can learn more about the psychological process of transition in William Bridges' *The Way of Transition: Embracing Life's Most Difficult Moments*,[20] while *Finding Yourself in Transition* by Robert Brumet[21] explores more specifically the spiritual opportunities inherent in life's changes. Two additional books that explore priestly spirituality and ministry in a changing church are Paul J Philibert's *Stewards of God's Mysteries*[22] and *Evolving Visions of the Priesthood* by Dean R. Hoge and Jacqueline E. Wenger.[23]

Resistance to Supervision

Many lay people trained in ministry will be familiar with pastoral supervision. For most clergy, it is a new word. However, with future demands for accountability, evaluation, and professionalism, supervision will become more sought after and will hopefully become a necessary requirement for those involved in ministry. At the same time it will be resisted.

Ryan LaMothe believes that the single most common motivation for avoiding supervision "is the fear of being vulnerable."[24] I find it ironic that clergy who minister to people who are vulnerable find it so hard to be vulnerable themselves. A healthy model of ministry is that of the wounded healer who is aware of personal weakness and struggle and can identify with others in their difficulties. To be vulnerable is to be real, to be strong, and it invites reflection which leads to growth. Those who are reluctant to engage in supervision need to be reminded of this.

A further resistance to supervision, founded on the belief that ministry is a vocation and not a profession, also needs to be addressed. Clergy have traditionally lived in a clerical culture that resists the notion of professionalism and all it entails.[25] For instance, the lack of structures of accountability, the placing of nearly all responsibility and decision-making power in the hands of clerics, the fact that "seminary formation still seems to turn out a great many priests of a conservative and even authoritarian and lone ranger mentality in regard to ministry,"[26] and an emphasis on control more than leadership,[27] might be described as symptoms of a clericalism that is unhealthy and does not promote self-reflection and reflective ministry.

In the transition that is currently going on in the church, clerical culture is being questioned and dismantled. My own bishop describes clericalism as a heresy. While I agree with him, I am aware, thanks to supervision, that often unconsciously I still live out of a clerical mindset. This has helped me be empathic yet challenging towards clergy who show resistance to pastoral supervision.

How do supervisors promote supervision to those who are resistant? Emphasizing the mutuality of the supervisory relationship can be useful in that supervisees start to realize that there is a sharing of power in the process, and a sharing of vulnerability. Group supervision with a number of priests who already trust each other, or who are of a similar age, or with clergy and lay ministers in a particular parish or deanery, might be beneficial. A group could form to examine particular aspects of ministry, for instance how the sacraments are celebrated in parishes, and then covenant to continue working together. I meet with a colleague monthly for lunch, followed by time when both of us talk about our ministry. Such peer supervision might be suggested to ministers as a useful form of ongoing formation. Helping ministers to see that pastoral supervision is essentially a support structure, and a learning partnership might also be helpful.

Conclusion

This chapter has argued that pastoral supervision needs to be an integrative process which honors the complexity of pastoral work and recognizes that ministry and the life of lay and clerical workers cannot be separated. It is a spiritual process sensitive to the transitions that are part and parcel of church and ministerial life today. It offers a "space to play"[28] with different options and possibilities and theologies. Its value is clear in the story of Alex.

There is increasing realization within the priesthood, in particular, that ongoing, life-long formation is needed. In his apostolic exhortation *Pastores Dabo Vobis*, Pope John Paul II offers a holistic description of priestly formation that encompasses four aspects, namely human, intellectual, spiritual, and pastoral.[29] Pastoral supervision focuses on these four aspects and, as a consequence, it will be a rich form of ongoing formation in the future. As a means of self-care, accountability, and support, supervision is a source of human formation. In its educative and managerial functions, it is a source of pastoral, spiritual, and intellectual formation.[30]

Much needs to be done to educate those involved in ministry about the benefits and support to be had from regular, protected time for reflection on practice with a person trained in pastoral supervision. As Pohly notes, "Many persons in ordained ministry are denied the benefit of regular professional evaluation. The result frequently is either frustration and eventual attrition from the ministry or the perpetuation of ineffective pastoral performance."[31] While educating those in ministry about pastoral supervision is challenging, perhaps the best advertisement for its successful adoption will be supervisors who are sensitive to the needs of pastoral workers, whose work will help eyes to open and hearts to burn again (Luke 24:31–32).

Notes

[1]Ministry is best seen as both profession and vocation. See Richard M. Gula, *Just Ministry: Professional Ethics for Pastoral Ministers* (New York: Paulist Press, 2010). However, there are twin dangers: over professionalizing can result in a certain minimalist approach while over spiritualising can result in neglecting professional obligations. In relation to these issues, and in regards to others which will become important as priesthood is seen as a profession (e.g., accountability, power in professional relationships, dual relationships, standards, evaluation, and ongoing education), see Richard M. Gula, *Ethics in Pastoral Ministry* (New York: Paulist Press, 1996).

[2]Such a process would include the three main functions of supervision as described by Kadushin, namely, educative, supportive, and managerial. See Peter Hawkins and Robin Shohet, *Supervision in the Helping Professions: An Individual, Group and Organizational Approach* (2nd. ed.; Maidenhead: Open University, 2003), 50.

[3]John Shea, *The Spiritual Wisdom of the Gospels for Christian Preachers and Teachers: Year A* (Collegeville, MN: Lithurgical Press, 2004). 170.

[4]Kenneth Pohly, *Transforming the Rough Places: The Ministry of Supervision* (2nd. ed.; Franklin, TN: Providence House Publishers, 2001), 107–8.

[5]"Lumen Gentium," in *Vatican II: The Conciliar and Post Conciliar Documents*, Austin Flannery, ed. (Dublin, Ireland: Dominican Publications, 1980; reprint, 5), No 28.

[6]John Foskett and David Lyall, *Helping the Helpers: Supervision and Pastoral Care, New Library of Pastoral Care* (London: SPCK, 1988), 32–41.

[7]Jane Leach and Michael Patterson, eds., *Pastoral Supervision: A Handbook* (London: SCM Press, 2010).

[8]Kirk Byron Jones, *Rest in the Storm: Self-Care Strategies for Clergy and Other Caregivers* (Valley Forge, PA: Judson Press, 2001).

[9]After Action Reviews focus on the following four sets of questions: 1. What were our intended results? (What was planned?); 2. What were our actual results? (What really happened?); 3. What caused our results? (Why did it happen?); 4. What will we sustain? Improve? (What can we do better next time?). For more information, see www.nelh.nhs.uk/knowledge_management/km2/aar_toolkit.asp and http://www.nwlink.com/~donclark/leader/leadaar.html

[10]Michael Carroll and Margaret Tholstrup, *Integrative Approaches to Supervision* (London: Jessica Kingsley, 2001), 77.

[11]James D. Whitehead and Evelyn Eaton Whitehead, *Method in Ministry: Theological Reflection and Christian Ministry* (New York: The Seabury Press, 1981), ix.

[12]Ibid. Instead of cultural resources, Coll talks about "wisdom and knowledge available . . . from philosophy . . . science, social sciences, and the arts." See Regina Coll, *The Heart and Soul of Parish Ministry* (Mystic, CT: Twenty-Third Publications, 2002), 11.

[13]Whitehead and Whitehead, *Method in Ministry*, 13.

[14]Patricia O'Connell Killen and John DeBeer, *The Art of Theological Reflection* (New York: Crossroad, 1995), 21.

[15]Conroy focuses on processing "inner experiences of spiritual directors that are evoked during direction sessions in order to help them grow in awareness of their reactions and responses, to allow them to respond in a God-centred and interiorly free manner, and to maintain a contemplative focus." See Maureen Conroy, *Looking into the Well: Supervision of Spiritual Directors* (Chicago: Loyola Press, 1995), 13.

[16]Ibid., 40.

[17]James Zullo describes transitions as "those normal turning points in human life that mark the passage between endings and beginnings, and which are characterized by a threefold movement: from one stable state or self-definition, into an in-between time of increased vulnerability and heightened potential, and toward a new or modified self-definition or life situation." See James R Zullo, "Navigating Transitions," *The Works* Winter (2001): 19.

[18]Zullo, "Navigating Transitions," 19.

[19]Zullo, "Navigating Transitions," 20.

[20]William Bridges, *The Way of Transition: Embracing Life's Most Difficult Moments* (Cambridge, MA: Perseus Publishing, 2001).

[21]Robert Brumet, *Finding Yourself in Transition: Using Life's Changes for Spiritual Awakening* (Unity City, MO: Unity Books, 1995).

[22]Paul J. Philibert, *Stewards of God's Mysteries: Priestly Spirituality in a Changing Church* (Collegeville, MN: Liturgical Press, 2004).

[23]Dean Hoge and Jacqueline E. Wenger, *Evolving Visions of the Priesthood: Changes from Vatican II to the Turn of the New Century* (Collegeville, MN: Liturgical Press, 2003).

[24]Ryan LaMothe, "A Challenge to Church Leaders: The Necessity of Supervision for Ordained Ministers," *The Journal of Pastoral Care & Counseling* 59, no. 1–2 (2005): 11.

[25]Cosgrove defines diocesan clerical culture as "a series of arrangements or structures which together constitute the institutional framework or system within which diocesan priests and bishops live and carry out their ministry. These structures and the diocesan clerical system which they make up have evolved over the centuries and are now for the most part supported and mandated by Church law and custom." See Bill Cosgrove, "The Diocesan Clerical System - 1: Institutional and Sociological Influences on the Diocesan Priest," *Doctrine and Life* 55, no. 8 (2005): 6.

[26]Bill Cosgrove, "The Diocesan Clerical System - 2: Positive and Negative Effects on the Clergy," *Doctrine and Life* 55, no. 9 (2005): 22.

[27]Ibid., 23.

[28]Frances Ward, *Lifelong Learning: Theological Education and Supervision* (London: SCM Press, 2005), 88.

[29]Pope John Paul II, *Pastores Dabo Vobis* (London: Catholic Truth Society, 1992), 116–60.

[30]The goals of pastoral supervision as defined by Pohly contains the four aspects of priestly formation outlined by John Paul II, namely self-awareness (human formation), ministering competence (pastoral formation), theological understanding (intellectual formation), and Christian commitment (spiritual formation).

[31]Pohly, *Transforming the Rough Places*, 86.

Bibliography

Bridges, William. *The Way of Transition: Embracing Life's Most Difficult Moments.* Cambridge, Massachusetts: Perseus Publishing, 2001.

Brumet, Robert. *Finding Yourself in Transition: Using Life's Changes for Spiritual Awakening.* Unity City, MO: Unity Books, 1995.

Carroll, Michael, and Margaret Tholstrup. *Integrative Approaches to Supervision.* London: Jessica Kingsley, 2001.

Coll, Regina. *The Heart and Soul of Parish Ministry.* Mystic, CT: Twenty-Third Publications, 2002.

Conroy, Maureen. *Looking into the Well: Supervision of Spiritual Directors.* Chicago: Loyola Press, 1995.

Cosgrove, Bill. "The Diocesan Clerical System - 1: Institutional and Sociological Influences on the Diocesan Priest." *Doctrine and Life* 55, no. 8 (2005): 5–19.

———. "The Diocesan Clerical System - 2: Positive and Negative Effects on the Clergy." *Doctrine and Life* 55, no. 9 (2005): 13–26.

Dulles, Avery. *The Priestly Office: A Theological Reflection.* New York: Paulist Press, 1997.

Foskett, John, and David Lyall. *Helping the Helpers: Supervision and Pastoral Care, New Library of Pastoral Care.* London: SPCK, 1988.

Gula, Richard M. *Ethics in Pastoral Ministry.* New York: Paulist Press, 1996.

_____. *Just Ministry: Professional Ethics for Pastoral Ministers.* Paulist Press: New York, 2010.

Hawkins, Peter, and Robin Shohet. *Supervision in the Helping Professions: An Individual, Group and Organizational Approach.* 2nd. ed. Maidenhead: Open University, 2003.

Hoge, Dean, and Jacqueline E Wenger. *Evolving Visions of the Priesthood: Changes from Vatican II to the Turn of the New Century.* Collegeville, MN: Liturgical Press, 2003.

Jones, Kirk Byron. *Rest in the Storm: Self-Care Strategies for Clergy and Other Caregivers.* Valley Forge, PA: Judson Press, 2001.

Killen, Patricia O'Connell, and John DeBeer. *The Art of Theological Reflection.* New York: Crossroad, 1995.

LaMothe, Ryan. "A Challenge to Church Leaders: The Necessity of Supervision for Ordained Ministers." *The Journal of Pastoral Care & Counseling* 59, no. 1–2 (2005): 3–15.

Leach, Jane, and Michael Patterson, eds. *Pastoral Supervision: A Handbook.* London: SCM Press, 2010.

"Lumen Gentium." Pages 340–426 in *Vatican II: The Conciliar and Post Conciliar Documents.* Edited by Austin Flannery. Dublin, Ireland: Dominican Publications, 1980. Reprint, 5.

Neuger, Christine Cozad, and James Newton Poling, eds. *The Care of Men.* Nashville: Abingdon Press, 1997

Philibert, Paul J. *Stewards of God's Mysteries: Priestly Spirituality in a Changing Church.* Collegeville, MN: Liturgical Press, 2004.

Pohly, Kenneth. *Transforming the Rough Places: The Ministry of Supervision.* 2nd.ed. Franklin, TN: Providence House Publishers, 2001.

Pope John Paul II. *Pastores Dabo Vobis.* London: Catholic Truth Society, 1992.

Shea, John. *The Spiritual Wisdom of the Gospels for Christian Preachers and Teachers: Year A: On Earth as It Is in Heaven.* Vol. 1 of *The Spiritual Wisdom of the Gospels for Christian Preachers and Teachers.* Collegeville, MN: Liturgical Press, 2004.

Ward, Frances. *Lifelong Learning: Theological Education and Supervision.* London: SCM Press, 2005.

Whitehead, James D., and Evelyn Eaton Whitehead. *Method in Ministry: Theological Reflection and Christian Ministry.* New York: The Seabury Press, 1981.

Zullo, James R. "Navigating Transitions." *The Works.* Winter (2001): 18–21.

Chapter

5

❧

Supervision in
Clinical Pastoral Education

❧ *Yuko Uesugi* ❧

I n a seminary class a professor asks, "How would you respond to a request of a mother who has just had fetal demise to have her 'baby' baptized?" Gina, one of the students in the class, answers, "A fetus is not a 'baby.' Also, this fetus is dead, therefore not a human. Sacraments are for living humans. In the same way that I cannot baptize this table at which I am sitting, I cannot baptize the fetus. Therefore, I would tell the mother that I won't baptize the fetus."

Gina's answer may be deemed theoretically and logically sound. Some may find this answer even theologically sound. But when a CPE supervisor heard this answer, it seemed to lack something extremely foundational. The supervisor asked Gina a question: "Would you, as a pastor, have the heart to offer this explanation to this grief-smitten mother who has just lost her fetus whom she had carried in her womb for eight months, and whom she perceived as her own beloved baby, whose loss was as devastating to her as the loss of a any other child for a mother?"[1]

What is Clinical Pastoral Education?

In the 1920s Richard C. Cabot conceived of clinical pastoral education (CPE) as a method of learning pastoral practice in a clinical setting under supervision. He was convinced that clergy should be trained to practice theology in the same way that physicians learn to practice medicine. He urged theological students to get clinical experience outside their lecture rooms "where they could visit the sick, the insane, the prisons, and the almshouses to practice theology where it is most needed." Anton T. Boisen enlarged the concept to include a case study method of theological inquiry—a study of "living human documents." William S. Keller began supervising theological students

---

[1] This and all other vignettes in this chapter are fictional accounts.

in case study methods, believing pastoral practice was complete only as it addressed contributing social conditions. As CPE developed, other leaders integrated knowledge from medicine, psychology, and other behavioral sciences into pastoral practice.

In CPE, theological students and ministers are brought into supervised encounters with persons in crisis. Out of an intense involvement with persons in need and the feedback from peers and supervisors, students develop new awareness of themselves as persons and of the needs of those to whom they minister. Any helping act of the students—whether a comment, a question, an action, a response, a feeling of internal judgment, or an overall attitude—becomes a subject for evaluation according to its effect upon the patient. Through theological reflection on specific human situations, students gain a new understanding of ministry and a different understanding of how theological knowledge functions in the caring process. The student's personal beliefs and theological understanding are the substance of what is done or acted out in the process of pastoral care, very much as the medical knowledge of a physician is employed to inform the procedures of treatment. CPE programs assist students to develop their awareness of themselves as ministers and of the ways they affect those to whom they minister. Since effective learning takes place when students reflect on their pastoral care practices—including their strengths and limitations—and become more conscious of their learning needs in the context of an authentic, relational, communal learning environment, I see my role as a supervisor as assisting students in the development of their awareness as persons and as spiritual caregivers, as they seek to enhance their competence in ministry.

To provide an understanding of how CPE programs assist students in their learning and growth, I will outline how I supervise students during a single unit of the full-time CPE program at UCLA Health System.

Selection of CPE Students

First of all, a careful admission process is essential. Given that CPE training is professional training, it is important to ascertain the student's readiness for intensive learning. In our student selection process, we evaluate students' *readiness* and *openness* for learning by assessing their level of self-awareness in terms of personal and pastoral identity, their level of pastoral skill and competence, their emotional maturity and availability, their ability to admit what they don't know and when they make mistakes, and their ability to be vulnerable with others in seeking consultation and feedback. We also assess the students' value systems, coping mechanisms, possible transference and counter-transference issues, and level of comfort with their emotional dynamics. We also assess the students' pastoral competences, including their level of empathy and their ability to provide spiritual care that is respectful and sensitive to the patients' and families' faith traditions. We also need to be certain that students understand and are willing to work within the interfaith context and the diverse population that are endemic to the CPE program at the UCLA Health System.

The supervisory relationship and bonding begin even before the admission interview. When students apply to CPE, most of them feel some level of anxiety as they are about to plunge into a new situation that demands much learning. Therefore, from the initial inquiry, I intentionally provide students with a lot of information and always invite them to contact me if they have further questions. This is one of my attempts to make the CPE learning environment as hospitable as possible for the prospective students, and to ease their anxieties by giving information that they need. During the interview, I use examples from real situations that occur in the hospital and ask the student how she imagines herself responding to such situations. Also, the interview time is not only for the supervisor to select the students who are suitable to our CPE program, but also for the students to select the suitable training center for their learning. A student like Gina described in my vignette may find that the UCLA Health System's interfaith context requires too great an accommodation and, as a consequence, decides that the UCLA Health System may not be the right fit for her. On the other hand, if she is motivated to learn by being stretched in this challenging context, then the UCLA Health System may be the right training center for her.

During her interview the CPE supervisor asked Gina, "During one of your on-call shifts, you are called to Labor and Delivery. A patient just had a fetal demise, and would like you to baptize her "baby." How would you imagine yourself as the chaplain responding to the mother's request?" Gina paused. This time, being in the hospital, the question felt more real for her than a hypothetical theological exercise in class. This was a real possibility for her to face and she would need to deal with a real person. Gina continued to pause, thought about the situation, and slowly answered, "Well . . . I would imagine that the patient is in great grief and pain. So, I would go there and see her and I would try to find a way to comfort her, and if she so desires, I would pray for her baby and bless the baby. I still don't know exactly how I could go about baptizing a baby who is not alive, but that's something I want to think more about." In Gina's response the supervisor saw Gina demonstrate her openness and willingness to face a new situation and learn. Gina was accepted into the program.

Supervising CPE Students

Once the supervisor invites a student into the program and the student accepts, a working alliance—which is the foundation of a supervisor-student relationship—begins to form. Since the supervisor's interactions and responses with students during the initial stage of their supervisor-student relationship are crucial in laying the groundwork for effective working alliances, I do my best to make myself available during the first week of the CPE program. Since students usually enter the new environment of the CPE program with high levels of anxiety, it is important to provide students with stability and information to ease their anxiety. Also, for some students, this CPE program may be the first time they have visited a person in a hospital room. Didactic orientation seminars cover topics such as "Initiating Spiritual Care Visits and Active Listening Skills," "Pastoral Care Responses," and "Chaplain Role Plays" to help students in dealing with their initial anxiety.

On the second day of the orientation, students begin working in their peer group to begin establishing a learning environment that is relational and communal. As students get acquainted with the new environment and their anxiety decreases, they are invited to share their life stories as a way to begin learning about, and from, each other. Because one of CPE's objectives is to assist students in increasing their self-awareness, I—in sharing my life story as a supervisor—model reflecting in describing how my past relationships and experiences have shaped my present value and belief systems, my attitudes, and my interpersonal relational styles. By inviting students to share their life stories, I encourage them to share as much as they feel comfortable sharing, so that the students begin to feel a sense of control and responsibility in their own learning experience. Also, as we begin our group sharing, I share my viewpoint that the group is a learning community, in contrast to the competitive learning environments with which most of the students are more familiar from their academic experiences. The expectations for the group members to be respectful of one another and to keep the group discussion confidential are emphasized, so that the students begin to learn the group's boundaries and to have a sense of safety.

After the story sharing, the students do a "transition exercise" with reflective questions, such as "what is my greatest fear for the CPE program" and "what is my greatest hope for my CPE experience." Through this exercise the students are invited to begin a direct experience of the CPE learning process. Each question is followed by a moment of silence. During the silent moment, I encourage them to pay attention to their internal dynamics and to become more aware of their internal voices, feelings, thoughts, and bodily sensations. After the silent moment, I invite the students to share their reflections as much as they feel comfortable sharing. By the end of the exercise, students have clearer ideas about their learning goals for this CPE unit. Since feeling often emerges in a significant learning process, this exercise is used so students can begin to open up the internal space for not only rational thoughts but also for feelings and intuitions. By having a moment to pause after each question, students are invited to reflect internally to see what is going on within them and to discover the clarity silence often brings. By taking time for reflection, students become more aware that the answer for their learning often dwells within themselves rather than coming from external sources such as a teacher or a supervisor.

To assist the students' transition from the more familiar academic learning model to CPE's experience-based learning model, I teach students the theories supporting CPE's action-reflection-action and conscious-competence models of learning. Using the conscious-competence learning model, I emphasize that being aware of one's learning needs (consciously incompetent) is already the second stage of one's learning journey—thus possibly decreasing the students' sense of shame for not knowing.

After the "transition exercise" and the initial didactic seminars, the students visit patients in their assigned units on the fourth day of the orientation. For some students, this may be the first time that they have visited patients in the hospital. In addition, they understand the expectation that they will be visiting patients as chaplains, even though they are still unsure about what they are supposed to do. Needless to say, the level of their anxiety can be extremely high.

One hour after the students were sent to their assigned units to begin visiting their patients, Gina came back into the supervisor's office in tears. The supervisor said, "Hi, Gina. What's going on?" By asking the question rather casually, the supervisor conveyed to Gina a sense of normalcy. "This is so hard. I cannot do this!" Gina began to cry. The supervisor gently closed the door of her office, invited Gina to have a seat, and waited until she calmed down. Once Gina had calmed down, the supervisor asked again, "What's going on? What happened?" This time Gina was a little more able to articulate. "I went to my assigned unit, tried to visit patients." The supervisor continued to provide Gina with her empathy and support through eye contact, facial expression, and nodding. Feeling accepted and affirmed, Gina continued. "But, when I got closer to the first patient's room, I got so scared and couldn't go any further." The supervisor asked, "What were you so scared of?" Gina: "I don't know." In order to help Gina identify the trigger(s) of her fear, the supervisor asked a more specific question, "It's OK, Gina. Let's think together. Could you tell me a little more about what you saw in the unit, what you thought or felt when you were in the unit?" Gina replied, "There were so many patients in the units. I saw their families at bedsides, and some of them were very upset and looked sad. When I saw them, I felt so overwhelmed and helpless. I really didn't know what to do. And then, I thought that I have 10 more weeks to go, and I got so scared." Gina cried with less emotional intensity. The supervisor continued to empathize with her: "I see lots of feelings and thoughts were going on for you. And I can imagine that was really hard. When you were in the unit, was there anything that reminded you of something from your past experiences or of someone you know?" Gina thought about the questions for a while and replied, "I was in a multiple-vehicle accident when I was in high school. I was OK, but I saw so many people suffering and in pain." With the supervisor's help, Gina processed her emotional reaction during her unit visit in relation to her experience of the accident. Gina became more able to understand the impact of the experience on her perception of her ministry. Afterwards, the supervisor also helped Gina make some specific plans to make her feel more comfortable in her assigned units. Through this supervisory intervention, the supervisor was able to help Gina regain her sense of control and self-confidence so she could return to her assigned units.

CPE's action-reflection-action model of learning can happen even before the students visit patients. In the face of real encounters with patients and their families, students become more aware of their unconscious expectation of themselves as persons and as ministers. Sometimes students get stuck between their unrealistic expectation of themselves and their perception of their own limitations. In such cases, these unconscious expectations need to be identified and evaluated before students can move forward. Also, encountering patients' pain and suffering may trigger some students' unresolved grief issues. In these cases, it is important for the supervisor to pay close attention to how the students are coping with their own grief.

Gina continued to make herself feel more comfortable in her assigned unit by getting to know the nursing and other medical staff, and she was slowly making progress in her patient visits as well.

In the full-time CPE program at the UCLA Health System, weekly **Verbatim Seminars** are scheduled in which students share presentations about one of their patient visit experiences with the group. Practices to ensure confidentiality and practices of patients' identity are observed. Students are asked to write in advance their reflections on their feelings, spiritual assessment, theological implications, evaluation of their pastoral care practices, and learning questions raised by this experience. Students learn whenever they realize their incompetence and limitations and shift from the *unconsciously incompetent* stage to the *consciously incompetent* stage. Reflection, evaluation, and receiving feedback from others are central to the learning process. The structure of the verbatim seminar very effectively supports the students' clinical pastoral learning experiences by focusing their peers' and supervisor's reflections on data from specific pastoral care encounters.

In the fourth week, Gina presented her second verbatim. In her verbatim she presented a case she encountered in the evening when she was on call. During one of her evening shifts, Gina was requested to assist a viewing for a Vietnamese Catholic couple whose baby had just died. In the early part of her visit, Gina tried to comfort the couple by offering prayer, offering to call a Catholic priest on their behalf, and by pastoral conversation—to all of which the couple was not receptive. The couple was very distraught and openly expressed their grief throughout the viewing. Gina stayed with the couple for the entire viewing (approximately three hours), and felt completely useless because she could not speak their language and they did not speak much English. The only thing she could do was watch the couple grieve and feel sad for them. Nonetheless, as they left the viewing, the couple was very appreciative to Gina for being there for them.

During the verbatim presentation, Gina expressed her frustration in her inability to provide spiritual care to the couple. She perceived herself as incompetent, useless, and helpless as a chaplain because she couldn't say or do anything to comfort the couple. The supervisor asked Gina why she thought the couple was appreciative for Gina at the end of the viewing. Gina responded, "Oh, they were really nice people." During this verbatim presentation, the supervisor invited the group members to reflect on their own experiences of loss and grief and what they found most comforting and helpful in dealing with their own grief process. During this session, Gina became more aware of her ministry style which focused heavily on doing and saying the right things for patients. Through reflection on this pastoral encounter in the group and by receiving feedback from her peers and supervisor, Gina also learned the power of her pastoral presence, for which the couple was so grateful.

Into CPE programs students bring what they have learned from their past experiences and relationships. Because they have frequently become "unconsciously competent," students forget that what they have learned often occurred in a particular situation to meet a particular need. Unless they become conscious about it, they may continue applying the old learning to a new situation even though the situation is quite different and requires a new way of responding. Students may become conscious of their learning needs when their routine responses produce surprising, unexpected outcomes. Accordingly, students are encouraged to pay attention to situations in which they don't know how to respond or are unsure about the effectiveness of their pastoral practices. Also, depending upon their internal resources (such as emotional maturity, openness to learning, ability to become vulnerable with others, and internal security), students differ in their capacity and pace of learning. Therefore, it is important for the supervisor to respect each student's readiness for learning and learning speed.

Each student also facilitates at least one **Story Theology** session. During this session, students share a story or vignette from part of their own life. After hearing the story, the group reflects upon it: first, by sharing immediate thoughts and personal associations; second, by sharing their observations and impressions of the storyteller; and third, by moving to theological and spiritual themes. The premise of this seminar is that all of life has a theological and spiritual dimension. This process also parallels patient visits where, as chaplains, students seek to discover the theological and spiritual dimensions of patients' stories. This exercise also helps students to become more aware of their internal dynamics and how their own experiences can help or hinder their ability to hear and connect with the storyteller.

CPE peer groups provide a rich learning environment where, as they support and challenge each other, students can become more conscious about their pastoral functioning and identity. By offering feedback and critique, and by identifying and understanding what happened, what worked or did not work and why, students can increase their awareness of their interpersonal styles, behaviors, responses, and reactions, and can adopt new models of effective relational patterns and responses.

An **Open Agenda Learning Seminar** is scheduled for one hour each week. This is time set aside without a pre-set agenda, where students assume responsibility for bringing learning agendas, issues, and questions related to the program, including interpersonal relationships within the CPE group, and ministry with patients and families. The open agenda learning seminar inherently treats the students as adult learners who are capable of self-direction and thus the group members are to share themselves and learn from one another. If necessary, I—as a supervisor—might invite group members to share their thoughts, help facilitate peer-helping connections or peer conflict resolution, and highlight the pastoral care issues being raised.

In addition to the above mentioned seminars, within the Spiritual Care Department of the UCLA Health System **Interfaith Spiritual Reflection** is held regularly. Leadership of these meetings is rotated among the CPE students, staff chaplains, and the supervisors. The purpose of the reflection time is to help ground the group members in their spiritual heritage, to help create a sense of spiritual community in the group, and to give students practice at creating and facilitating services in an interfaith context. Participants fill out an evaluation form at the end of the reflection time to give the leader(s) constructive feedback.

In our CPE program **Individual Supervisory Conferences** (ISCs) are scheduled for each student weekly. This is not the only time that students can access their supervisor, but is guaranteed time set aside for supervisory consultation and reflection on the student's learning. In order to encourage students' ongoing self-reflection and self-direction, students are expected to reflect on their relationships with patients, families, staff, peers, supervisor, and self during the week, and to bring their reflection and agenda for their learning to their ISCs.

On the sixth week of the program, Gina came to her ISC feeling completely exhausted. She had had two evening on-call shifts during the previous week and had several emergency requests and patient deaths during these shifts. Also, two of her long-term patients died in the same week. As she came into the supervisor's office, Gina began to complain about how busy she had been and how exhausted she was feeling. Usually Gina viewed herself as a capable person who liked to push herself to the limit and attain high achievement in whatever she did, whether academia, competitive sports, or ministry. She was already aware of her tendency to overextend herself and aware of the cost of such overextension in the long run, but she was not able to slow down.

The supervisor assessed that Gina's drive for hard work was attributable to unconscious emotional needs. Gina equated her self-worth with her hard work and high achievement. Based on family systems theory, the supervisor understood that Gina learned to be a high achiever as a coping strategy acquired from her family of origin. The supervisor asked Gina where she thought she had received the message to be a high achiever. Gina told the supervisor that her parents always encouraged her to do her best, and when she didn't do well, there was always a clear message of disapproval.

A CPE program is very demanding and it stretches the student spiritually, emotionally, and physically. When the supervisor heard Gina's complaint, it became clear that the tension between Gina's value system and her physical and emotional exhaustion was forcing her to a new level of self-understanding and self-acceptance. The supervisor invited Gina to become aware of her unconscious belief that she is worthy and valuable only through her high achievement. Then the supervisor invited Gina to reflect on the truth, based on Gina's understanding of Christian theology, that all humanity is worthy to be loved by God—even in the absence of high achievement. Accordingly, the supervisor suggested that Gina seek to incorporate perceived weakness or limitation into an integral part of herself.

To counterbalance Gina's experience of her parents, the supervisor—as Gina's authority figure—decided to present a different response whenever Gina expressed her fatigue and weaknesses, and to be respectful and supportive of Gina's needs as much as possible. The supervisor acknowledged to Gina that being a high achiever gained her much praise from others around her, and empathized with her frustration with the physical exhaustion that forced her to slow down. To provide Gina with a nonjudgmental attitude and pastoral support for her slowing down, the supervisor used reflection on her own experience. Through sharing her own tendency for high achievement and its consequences in her life, the supervisor normalized Gina's emotional conflict. Reflecting on Christ's great commandments, where he commands his disciples to love their God with all their hearts, strength, and soul, and to love their neighbors as they love themselves, and recalling Christ's acceptance and love of persons, regardless of their status or achievements, Gina was invited to think how she could become more loving not only of God and of others, but also of herself.

Based on this experience, Gina revised one of her learning goals for the CPE unit from "improve my pastoral care skills and competence, and become a more effective spiritual caregiver" to "become more able to accept myself without overachieving and better take care of myself without feeling guilty." Gina processed her thoughts and feelings around this change, and received support from her peers and supervisor. Originally Gina was somewhat guarded and reluctant to ask for help from others. Based on her group theory, the supervisor understood that the peer group could be a place for students to learn how to receive and provide pastoral care for each other. The supervisor encouraged Gina to use not only her ISC but also her peer group for support and learning opportunities. By receiving support and empathy from others, Gina became more able to internalize their care and acceptance of her as a person, and she became better able to take care of her own needs. Also, as she became more able to take care of herself, Gina also became more patient and empathetic with others' needs for help.

A **Joint Patient Visit** is conducted at least once during the CPE unit with each student. The supervisor accompanies students during their patient visits and observes the students' pastoral interaction in the room. Right after the visits with patients (and sometimes with patients' families), the student and the supervisor sit down and discuss each visit. The supervisor asks the student to make a spiritual assessment of the patient, to reflect on the effectiveness of their pastoral care practices in that particular patient encounter, and if possible, their pastoral care plan for the patient going forward. After the student's self-evaluation, the supervisor gives the student feedback about the strengths and weaknesses that were observed during the visit. As with verbatim seminars, the supervisor and the student reflect on the student's effectiveness based on the concrete data from a specific pastoral encounter.

When Gina's supervisor did joint patient visits with her, she observed Gina avoided responding to patients' feelings even when patients brought them up in their conversation. Whenever it happened, Gina avoided responding by ignoring them or by changing the subject of the conversation. The supervisor assessed that Gina's avoidance of dealing with the patients' emotions was an unconscious, automatic emotional reaction, a coping mechanism that she had learned in her past. To help Gina become more conscious about her emotional reaction in her pastoral functioning, the supervisor shared her observation with Gina. As the supervisor shared her observation with Gina, she observed in Gina's facial expression and body language her strong anger and frustration, as well as an equally strong suppressing energy. Using "here-and-now" experience, the supervisor shared her current observation with Gina and invited her to reflect on it. As Gina identified and verified these feelings in herself, the supervisor invited Gina to go deeper with her feelings, and provided her with a pastoral presence as she tried to do so.

As Gina continued to reflect on her feelings with her supervisor, she became aware of profound grief over her lost childhood (due to her step-father's *emotional abuse), her strong anger, and her equally strong fear of anger. Gina was afraid not only of the anger that was expressed very destructively and violently by her step father, but also of her own anger which, once she let it come out, would become uncontrollable like her step-father's. The supervisor observed strong internal conflict in Gina and, based on her understanding of various personality theories, she determined that further exploration of this conflict would be beyond the scope of CPE. The supervisor shared her compassion for Gina, affirmed her courage to face her emotions, and expressed her appreciation for Gina's trust in choosing to become vulnerable with her. The supervisor assured Gina that she would continue to support her around this issue as much as she could, but also suggested that she might acquire professional support beyond CPE. Gina told the supervisor that she had been in counseling before and thought that it would be helpful for her to go back to her counselor for further assistance. Later, Gina found a counselor with whom she felt comfortable working.*

In clerical supervision, all supervisors wrestle with a tension between the desire to let supervisees learn by trial and error and the desire to ensure the highest quality of spiritual care the system can offer. In situations similar to Gina's, some supervisors may decide to intervene in the situations and respond to the patient's pastoral care needs, which the student seems to be unable to do. Such an intervention, being done in front of the student (modeling), can be an effective form of teaching. However, by taking over the learning tension of the student too quickly, the supervisor may curtail a teaching opportunity to have the student reflect on her limitations deeply. In CPE training, assisting the personal growth of students is an important goal. Students cannot engage in such close reflection upon their efforts to care for others without wrestling with personal changes in their own attitudes and behavior. Supervisors stimulate self-awareness in their supervisees, encouraging them to struggle with their internal conflicts as they work with others in their pastoral functioning. This is when the "art" part, the more intuition and more relationally responsive part, of clinical supervision needs to occur. However, in CPE, the supervisor's focus tends to fall more immediately on those internal conflicts that influence the student's pastoral functioning and their practice of spiritual care.

Students' Self-Evaluation on Their Learning Progress

Mid-Unit Evaluation is conducted in the sixth week. As was seen in the vignette about Gina, often mid-unit evaluation is a time for students to evaluate their learning progress and adjust the learning goals if necessary.

Final Evaluation is the time for students to evaluate their experiences and to begin integrating their learning into life beyond CPE. The students are required to complete a written final evaluation that is guided by ACPE's (Association of Clinical Pastoral Education) *Outcomes*. After students share their final evaluations in the group, the peers give the presenter their affirmations and challenges for future growth. After the students' final evaluation presentations, the supervisor also gives each student a professional evaluation based on ACPE's *Outcomes*. If the students and the supervisor are successful in maintaining an effective learning alliance, there will be little surprise in the final evaluation. If a student is surprised or disagrees with the supervisor's evaluation of their work, the ISC time is used to process their thoughts and feelings together.

Qualification and Training of the CPE Supervisor

Supervision in an educational setting involves more than ordinary teaching ability. "Supervision" designates an extended relationship in which an experienced clinician helps trainees to increase their competence in the pastoral role by reflecting on the concrete process of pastoral caregiving. It calls for special skills in enabling others to observe for themselves, to draw their own conclusions, to make their own applications of theory to practice, and to grow as persons in the process. In Supervisory CPE the student learns the theory and practice of supervision and has an experience of supervising other CPE students under the guidance of and with the consultation of a CPE supervisor.

Because supervisory theory greatly impacts the way a supervisor teaches and supervises students, it is crucial that supervisors identify and articulate their understanding of clinical pastoral supervision.

Therefore, in its certification process, ACPE includes in its *standards* the following competences as necessary for a successful CPE supervisor:

Competence as a Pastoral Supervisor

❯ maintain personal integrity and a deepening pastoral identity,

❯ demonstrate emotional and spiritual maturity,

❯ form meaningful pastoral relationships,

❯ self-supervise [one's] own on-going pastoral practice,

❯ refines one's professional identity as a clinical pastoral educator,

❯ demonstrate awareness of how one's culture affects professional and personal identity, pastoral practice, the supervisory relationship, and student learning.

Competence in the Theories of Supervision

❯ articulate understanding of and methodology for clinical pastoral supervision based on a critical grasp of the professional literature relating to the field of clinical supervision,

❯ articulate and implement a philosophy of CPE based on an educational model integrating the theory and practice of CPE, which is based on and congruent with one's theology,

❯ articulate rationale for multicultural competence, integrating the theory and practice of CPE, which is based on and congruent with one's theology.

Competence in the Practice of CPE Supervision

❯ assess an individual student's learning patterns, personality, religious history, and cultural values as a basis for supervisory strategies,

❯ supervise students' pastoral work, giving attention to unique patterns of personal and professional development, including the ability to assist students' movement toward pastoral identity,

❯ define and evaluate students' pastoral and personal resources, and use supervisory strategies and interventions to facilitate students' learning and development in pastoral care,

❯ assist students in taking responsibility for formulating a learning process and evaluating the results of the learning experience,

❯ use one's personality and personal, religious, and cultural history as a teaching resource in shaping a personal supervisory style,

❯ facilitate development of group interpersonal interaction,

❯ enable students to use their responses to the program as a learning experience.

Competence in CPE Program Design and Implementation

❯ develop and organize programs of CPE based on program educational principles appropriate to experiential learning,

❯ manage CPE programs effectively,

❯ develop a variety of CPE program resources,

❯ use diverse clinical educational methods,

❯ work with the theological implications of the ministry context,

❯ understand and apply professional organizational ethics as they relate to CPE and pastoral practice,

❯ use appropriate clinical skills and teaching methods that integrate the role of context and culture in pastoral practice and education,

❯ advocate for students based on awareness of how persons' social locations, systems, and structures affect one's ministry, learning and the educational context,

❯ consider cultural factors in the use of learning assessments, educational strategies, curriculum resources, and evaluation procedures.

Competence in Pastoral Education

❯ integrates educational theory, knowledge of behavioral science, professional and organizational ethics, theology, and pastoral identity into supervisory function,

❯ demonstrate awareness of the cultural context of diverse student groups and clinical populations that integrates and articulates ethnic identity development and its implications for pastoral practice and supervisory relationships.

Conclusion

This chapter demonstrates supervisory theories and interventions using the example of the UCLA Health System's CPE program. Within ACPE's standards, there is considerable room for a variety of supervisory practices based on an individual supervisor's theoretical foundation. In ACPE's CPE certification process, supervisors are expected to become learners of theology, educational theories, and personality theories to inform their supervisory work. Also, CPE supervisors are expected to go through intensive and extensive inner work so that they become more aware of who they are as persons and as pastoral educators.

As a CPE supervisor I see my role as accompanying students on their learning journeys by assisting them in their development of self-awareness, pastoral identity, and pastoral competence. In order to do so, I facilitate a community that encourages mutual learning and draws out the potential of each student by allowing them to expand their horizons and integrate new understandings of self, others, and God. Therefore, in my supervisory practice I focus on the students' growth towards wholeness as persons and spiritual caregivers by encouraging them to increase their self-awareness and self-acceptance by acknowledging weaknesses and limitations, and by integrating their theology into their individual lives and ministries.

Bibliography

Association for Clinical Pastoral Education. *2010 Standards*. www.acpe.edu
_____. *Who We Are*. www.acpe.edu

Augsburger, David. *Pastoral Counseling Across Cultures*. Philadelphia: The Westminster Press, 1986.

Bowen, Murray. *Family Therapy in Clinical Practice*. Northvale: Jason Aronson, 1986.

Brock, Rita Nakashima. *Journeys by Heart: A Christology of Erotic Power*. New York: Crossroad, 1988.

Brueggemann, Walter. *The Message of Psalms*. Minneapolis: Augsburg, 1984.

Corey, Marianne Schneider and Gerald Corey. *Groups: Process and Practice*, 6th ed. Pacific Grove: Brooks/Cale Publishing Co., 1992.

Ekstein, Rudolf and Robert Wallerstein. *The Teaching and Learning of Psychotherapy*, 2nd ed. New York: International Universities Press, 1972.

Fowler, James. *Stages of Faith: The Psychology of Human Development and the Quest for Meaning*. San Francisco: Harper and Row, 1981.

Friedman, Edwin H. *Generation to Generation: Family Process in Church and Synagogue.* New York: The Guilford Press, 1985.

The Holy Bible, New Revised Standard Version. Iowa Falls: World Bible Publishers, Inc., 1989.

Jung, Carl Gustav. *Modern Man in Search of Soul* San Diego: Harcourt. Inc., 1933.

_____. *Memories, Dreams, and Reflections*. New York: Vintage Books, 1965.

_____. *The Portable Jung*. New York: Penguin Books, 1971.

Knowles, Malcolm. *The Adult Learner: A Neglected Species*, 4th ed. Houston: Gulf Publishing, 1990.

Kwon, Soo-Young and Anthony Duc Le. "Relationship Building in Clinical Pastoral Education: A Confucian Reflection from Asian Chaplains." *The Journal of Pastoral Care and Counseling*, Fall 2004, Vol. 58, No. 3. 203–14.

Kruger, Justin, and David Dunning. "Unskilled and Unaware of It: How Difficulties in Recognizing One's Own Incompetence Lead to Inflated Self-Assessments." *Journal of Personality and Social Psychology*, 1999, Vol. 77, No. 6. 1121–34.

Merton, Thomas. *No Man Is an Island*. San Diego: Harcourt, Inc., 1955.

_____. *The Asian Journal of Thomas Merton*. New York: New Directions, 1975.

Nouwen, Henri. *The Wounded Healer: Ministry in Contemporary Society*. New York: Image Books, 1979.

_____. *In the Name of Jesus: Reflections on Christian Leadership*. New York: Crossroad, 1989.

_____. *Life of the Beloved: Spiritual Living in a Secular World*. New York: Crossroad, 1992.

Palmer, Parker. *To Know as We Are Known: Education as a Spiritual Journey*. San Francisco: HarperCollins, 1993.

_____. *The Courage To Teach: Exploring the Inner Landscape of a Teacher's Life*. San Francisco: Jossey-Bass Publishers, 1998.

Schön, Donald A. *Educating the Reflective Practitioner: Toward a New Design for Teaching and Learning in the Professions*. San Francisco: Jossey-Bass, 1987.

Steer, David A., ed. *The Supervision of Pastoral Care*. Louisville: Westminster/John Knox, 1989.

Stone, Charlsena F. "Exploring Cultural Competencies of Certified Therapeutic Recreation Specialists: Implications for Education and Training." *Therapeutic Recreation Journal*, Second Quarter 2003.

Sue, Derald Wing and David Sue. *Counseling the Culturally Different: Theory and Practice*, 2nd ed. New York: John Wiley & Sons, Inc., 1990.

Tillich, Paul. *The Dynamics of Faith*. New York: Harper and Row, 1957.

_____. *The Courage to Be*. New Haven: Yale University Press, 1958.

Yalom, Irwin D. *The Theory and Practice of Group Psychotherapy*, 4th ed. New York: Basic Books, 1995.

Chapter

6

∾

The Ministry of Supervision:

Call, Competency, Commitment

∾ *Maureen Conroy* ∾

This chapter is a further development of an article which first appeared in *Presence*, "An Interated Model of Supervision in Training Spiritual Directors" (Vol. 9, No. 1, 2003). Used with permission.

A   s the number of preparation programs for spiritual directors grows throughout the world, educators of spiritual directors are acutely aware of the need for competent supervisors. Traditionally, persons who are experienced spiritual directors adopt the role of supervisor. Although experience as a spiritual director is one of the greatest gifts people bring to the ministry of supervision, many supervisors ask themselves:

> ❯ What else do I need in order to be a competent supervisor and to enter fully into the ministry of supervision?
>
> ❯ Do I feel called to be a supervisor of spiritual directors?
>
> ❯ What does a commitment to this ministry involve?

This chapter reflects on the paradigm of supervision and explores three important dimensions about the growing ministry of supervision: call, competency, and commitment. It unfolds in the context of a group of supervisors meeting for a weekend to evaluate and prayerfully reflect on their supervisory work. Although the focus of this chapter is specifically on supervision for spiritual directors, the dimensions and dynamics discussed can be applied to all forms of supervision in ministry and other helping professions, such as psychological therapy.

A group of supervisors who recently completed conducting a two-year spiritual direction training program gathered for a Discernment Weekend to reflect on and refine the dimensions of the program. Knowing that supervision is the heartbeat of the program, they spent much time prayerfully pondering the paradigm and dynamics of their approach to supervision. Realizing how important it is to share a common vision, they contemplatively discerned each aspect of supervision and came up with the following dimensions.

The Paradigm of Supervision: Ministry, Mission, and Mystery

Supervision of spiritual directors is considered a "ministry." Like other ministries, it originates from a faith community, flows out of the charism of that community, and nourishes and expands the community. Rooted in God's presence and the gift of the Spirit, supervision strengthens spiritual directors' contemplative posture and abilities for discernment. Supervision enables directors to be vibrant messengers of God's gracious love for individuals and faith communities worldwide.

Second, supervision has a "mission" to help spiritual directors grow in self-awareness, interior freedom, and the ability to help others enter deeply into a rich experience of God's loving presence. It assists directors to notice blind spots and areas of resistance, vulnerability, and brokenness that prevent them from staying with their directees' life and spiritual experiences. Also, supervision helps spiritual directors to be in touch with God's lively presence during direction sessions so that they, in turn, can help directees linger with their personal God.

Thirdly, supervision is permeated with a sense of "mystery," the mystery of God moving in the hearts and minds of spiritual directors while companioning others. During the supervision process, directors are invited into the holy mystery of surrendering to God's woundedness and unfreedom so that they can journey with others into strength and freedom. They are encouraged to expose areas of blindness and darkness to God so that they can be transformed into gifts of truth and enlightenment.

Supervision, like spiritual direction, is a God-centered experience, an experience of contemplation and discernment. The atmosphere of supervision sessions is meant to be permeated with a sense of reverence, awe, and the privilege of companioning others in such a sacred way. The term "supervision," which originates from the helping professions of counseling and therapy, can sound clinical and directive. Although precise skills and education are needed, supervision is also an inspired art of enlightenment and a learned skill of empowerment. It is the skill of uncovering areas of unfreedom and giftedness in spiritual directors so that those directors can more readily facilitate God's lively presence in the persons they companion. Supervision is the art of allowing the mystery of God's transforming grace to move deeply into their own hearts as they journey with others.

The Quality of the Call

The supervision team spent time prayerfully pondering the unique call to supervision. Also, because they had become well-known as a high-quality supervisory team, they discussed questions that were being addressed to them by other supervisors and educational programs. They were delighted to have this prayerful time to reflect on specific dimensions of a call to be a supervisor and to prayerfully ponder their own unique call. They entered into the following prayer experience as a basis for their unfolding discernment.

Discerning the Call to the Ministry of Supervision

Enter into a contemplative inner space. Be aware of God's presence with you as you ponder your call to the ministry of supervision. What are your attractions, the drawings of your heart to this ministry? What are your desires, your feelings? Notice the various pulls and counter-pulls of your spirit. How would you describe them?

Be attentive to and linger with God's presence in your attractions. What is God's presence like? God's desires? God's heart? How is God looking at you now?

What gifts do you bring to this ministry? What gifts does God focus on? What gifts need to be strengthened? What graces do you need? How do you need God to be with you?

What specific circumstances are drawing you to this ministry? How does this attraction fit your experience of God, life, and ministry?

What background and preparation do you bring? What further preparation do you need?

In your imagination, heart, and spirit, envision yourself offering supervision. How do you see yourself concretely living out this call? Where and with whom do you see yourself offering this ministry? What is God's presence like there?

What is your inner stance like: free? unfree?

What inner attitudes do you need in order to follow this call? What outer realities do you need to let go of, for example, another dimension of your ministry?

In what ways will you seek confirmation of your possible decision to follow the drawings of your heart?

How will you know that your decision is confirmed?

Supervision has the quality of a sacred call. Supervisors are called by God and a faith community to be "servants of the servants." They are called to facilitate other ministers—namely, spiritual directors—and to foster individuals' contemplation and growing relationship with God. They are "companions with other companions" in that they walk with spiritual directors as they companion people on their spiritual journey. Although the call to supervision must be confirmed by a faith community, it is rooted in outer circumstances and an inner attraction.

OUTER CIRCUMSTANCES

The outer dimension is the need for supervision in a given situation. This need emerges in different ways. One scenario is an individual in a training program for spiritual directors who must find a supervisor upon returning home. For example, the Christian Spirituality Program at Creighton University, Omaha, Nebraska—which educates people from all over the world—requires that those preparing for the ministry of spiritual direction receive at least one year of supervision during their practicum experience. Therefore, the students, upon arriving back home, seek out persons to supervise them with questions in mind such as: "Where do I find someone who is qualified to be my supervisor? How do I know that this person is qualified?"

A second scenario is that an experienced spiritual director is asked by a beginning director to be his or her supervisor. This person asks: "Do I have the gifts and knowledge to be a supervisor? Do I have enough background and experience to take on such a commitment? Where and from whom can I find support during this endeavor?"

A third possibility is that a group of spiritual directors realizes the need to develop a program to prepare spiritual directors in a given geographical area. Several important questions emerge in this type of situation, including: "Who will offer supervision? How will they be prepared to be supervisors?" These spiritual directors enter into a discernment and planning process around these and other questions related to developing a program.

A fourth scenario is that an institution such as a college, university, seminary, or retreat house discerns the need to begin a developmental program for spiritual directors and realizes the importance of gathering competent supervisors to walk with participants. Significant questions that need to be addressed are: "How will we go about finding supervisors? What criteria exist that qualify someone to be a supervisor?"

INNER ATTRACTION

Simultaneous with these outer circumstances is what occurs in the heart and spirit of those who may consider offering supervision. Individuals invited into the ministry of supervision feel a drawing of the heart, a desire to give what they have received: "The gift you have received, give as a gift" (Mt 10:8, NAB). Potential supervisors must have a deep love for and commitment to the ministry of spiritual direction. They must have a strong desire to help others to prepare for this ministry. Supervision is a call within a call, an amplification or expansion of the call to spiritual direction. Supervisors often experience a compelling attraction, pull, or movement of the heart to companion others as their gifts for spiritual direction unfold and their weaknesses are transformed by God's loving presence. They are drawn as wounded healers to accompany other wounded healers who are in love with God and the people of God.

The ministry of supervision is both grounded in and fosters a contemplative presence. As individuals discern their call to supervision, they need to be attentive to the presence of God in their own desires and attitudes as well as notice God's desires for them. They need to sift out the pulls and counter-pulls of their hearts as they pay attention to God's heart and their attraction to this ministry. Through a contemplative posture they discern whether the ministry of supervision is congruent with the grace they experience as spiritual directors. They create the space for the guiding presence of the Spirit to stir into flame the gifts needed to be a companion for other spiritual directors.

Confirmation

The call to supervision must be confirmed interiorly and exteriorly. As with other significant decisions to companion God's people through a specific ministry, supervisors experience inner confirmation by the fruits of the Spirit that are signaled by joy, peace, patience, and the fullness of heart they feel within. They experience a sense of rightness and truth that this call fits their experience as a spiritual director. They feel a deep desire to companion spiritual directors, a growing enthusiasm, and an expanding energy for service. Exteriorly, supervisors are being invited by a community of faith. Others are seeing their gifts to minister to spiritual directors in this way.

In sum, the call to supervision is a deep drawing of the heart in response to specific circumstances; it originates from a faith community and is for the service of God's people. An amplification of the call to spiritual direction, supervision is rooted in a deep desire that the gift of spiritual direction be available to many people in a given area. This call, like the call to spiritual direction, must be grounded in a contemplative atmosphere and discerned in a prayerful way. Attentiveness to God's desires as well as one's own attraction is essential in the discerning process. The call requires the confirmation of a community of faith, the sense of God's affirmation, and a sense of congruence between supervision and one's heart.

Competency

Just as many people enter programs to develop their gifts as spiritual directors, so too most supervisors need similar preparation to become supervisors. Their development as competent supervisors requires both inner and outer preparation.

Inner Readiness

The inner readiness of a supervisor is similar to that of becoming a spiritual director; however, a deepening and fine-tuning process takes place. Supervisors must have a well-developed contemplative stance in their life and ministry. They must be able to allow God to be the Primary Mover in their spiritual-direction ministry and to be attentive to God in every situation. Supervisors need to possess a fine-tuned ability to sift through their own and others' interior movements, a keen self-awareness, and a growing self-knowledge. They need to be deeply in touch with themselves as wounded healers, affectively aware of their own areas of darkness and vulnerability as well as their areas of freedom and strength.

Thus, the inner preparation of the supervisor includes:

❯ a well-developed contemplative stance in one's own heart and life,

❯ an ability to foster a contemplative approach and presence in spiritual direction,

❯ a fine-tuned ability to sift through one's own and others' spiritual movements,

❯ a keen self-awareness and self-knowledge,

❯ an awareness of oneself as a wounded healer in touch with one's own areas of unfreedom and vulnerability,

❯ a deep capacity for empathy and compassion.

Outer Preparation

The outer preparation for supervision includes sufficient experience as a spiritual director, adequate theoretical knowledge, and the development of specific skills. Recommended components include:

❯ a minimum of three years experience as a spiritual director,

❯ engagement in a great deal of individual supervision for oneself,

❯ participation in supervision—with a peer group,

❯ adequate knowledge of psychology, spirituality, relational skills, and group process,

❯ well-developed skills of listening, savoring, exploring, and responding,

❯ clear knowledge of the differences between supervision and consultation,

❯ participation in a training workshop for supervisors or involvement in a mentoring relationship with an experienced supervisor during the first several years of supervising.

The greatest gift that people bring to the ministry of supervision is the experience of:

❯ being aware of God's affective presence and awareness of one's own interior movements,

❯ offering spiritual direction for a significant period of time,

❯ being a recipient of much supervision.

The gift of experience, along with adequate knowledge of psychological and spiritual dynamics, enables spiritual directors to respond to the call of supervision with inner freedom and a sense of responsibility.

A question often arises: "Can someone who is a therapist who supervises other therapists also be a supervisor for spiritual directors?" Because supervision involves both a contemplative and discerning approach, the supervisor is usually an experienced spiritual director. However, there are circumstances in which the latter is not available, so the supervisor might be someone who supervises counselors and therapists.

Commitment

The supervisory team experienced the great amount of caring support, time, and energy that went into companioning each of the twelve graduates of the spiritual director's program. They felt a deep sense of satisfaction at the tremendous growth that occurred in each of the new spiritual directors. They now entered into a period of prayerful pondering, to consider the dynamics of their commitment as supervisors and to contemplate in God's loving presence their own growth as persons and supervisors.

Commitment to the ministry of supervision has several aspects:

> the initial "yes" to offer supervision and to be mentored during the first several years,

> a willingness to take the time to pray contemplatively about the experience of supervision and to reflect on one's own inner process while supervising,

> an investment in specific ways for ongoing growth such as periodic evaluation of one's abilities and regular gatherings with other supervisors to fine-tune the skills of supervision.

The Initial "Yes"

After carefully contemplating their possible call to supervision, spiritual directors may respond positively. They may gradually realize that they have the desire, background, experience, and abilities to enter into the ministry of supervision. Also, they often feel the need for mentoring by another experienced supervisor.

Joan, remembering when she said yes to being a supervisor in the program, said, "I felt honored to be invited by this well-known program, but I knew I could not do it alone. After carefully praying over your request, I said I would join you in supervising others only if I could meet with an experienced supervisor to review my work and my abilities. During the past two years, it was a huge blessing for me to meet with others on a regular basis to reflect on my work.

Jim shared something similar when he initially responded "yes" to the invitation to become a supervisor: "I can only say 'yes' if I am able to meet with an experienced supervisor to be 'supervised on my supervision.' I could not have done supervision without this tremendous support and skilled mentoring."

The group recalled that when they began this training program, "We agreed to participate in a five-day training program on supervision and to meet monthly to mentor one another on our work of supervision. How important those two decisions were for the development of our supervisory skills!"

Thus, supervisors make a commitment not only to be supervisors but also to engage in a mentoring experience that will facilitate the growth of their supervisory skills.

Praying with Supervision Experiences

When supervisors respond "yes" to the ministry of supervision, they also commit themselves to pray about their experiences of supervision and to reflect on their own inner process while supervising. Supervision, being both a contemplative and discerning experience, requires that supervisors adopt a prayerful stance toward their work with supervisees.

Supervisors, like spiritual directors, experience interior movements while supervising. They may be drawn into the supervisee's experience as it is unfolding, flowing freely with the affective experience as insights emerge and freedom grows. They may feel a vivid sense of God's presence and joyfully contemplate God's work in the interior space of the supervisee. However, supervisors may also feel a lack of engagement, agitation, frustration, boredom, and restlessness as those feelings are experienced and shared by the supervisee. As a consequence, supervisors may lose sight of God's permeating presence in the session. Therefore, supervisors must make a covenant agreement with God and themselves to process their own inner experience while supervising in a prayerful and honest way.

Looking into the Well: Supervision of Spiritual Directors develops an analogy between a well and the "inner well" of a spiritual director. During a supervision session, the spiritual director, supervisor, and God look contemplatively into the director's inner well of direction experiences, reverently drawing out and processing a direction experience and allowing the Living Waters of God's loving presence to seep into this experience. This analogy offers a way to process supervision experiences in a contemplative way. The excerpt below is from *Looking into the Well*, adapted from pages 213–14. (See also chapter 9, "The Supervisor's Discerning Heart.")

Go to the well of your supervision experiences. Contemplate each supervision session with God, asking God to give you a discerning heart as you contemplate together. Ask God to drench you in the life-giving waters of God's gracious presence and to provide insight into your gifts and concrete experience as a supervisor.

Let your heart rest with one supervision session. Notice the atmosphere, pace, and presence of the session.

Was there a contemplative atmosphere? Was there a discerning presence, an evocative approach, a slow or fast pace, a clear focus on the director's experience, or an in-depth exploration into significant movement and issues?

What was God's presence like?

As you ponder, reflect on the supervisee's experience of supervision. What issues emerged for him or her? Were there growing edges, resistances, struggles, joys, or frustrations?

Notice God's presence with the person, and ask God to continue to bless the supervisee's ministry of spiritual direction.

Be attentive to your inner experience during the session. What feelings arose within you? Were there struggles, joys, resistances, personal issues, or growing edges?

What was God's presence like for you as supervisor? Did you ask God for what you needed? Ask God to continue to be with you as you supervise.

Ask God for the necessary qualities that will enable you to be a contemplative and caring presence for this supervisee in future sessions.

As you contemplate and reflect, share with God any thoughts and feelings that may arise within you. Be attentive to God's presence with and response to you. Ask God to drench you and the person you are supervising in the Living Waters of God's love and life-giving presence.

Ongoing Growth as a Supervisor

After an inspiring group sharing on the fruits of their prayer, the group prayed with and shared about their own growth as supervisors. They prayed with the Reflection Instrument that they designed as the two-year program was unfolding. Again, they were deeply enriched by the honest and reverent group sharing. The Reflection Instrument included the following.

When supervisors commit themselves to the ministry of supervision, they also commit to their ongoing growth as supervisors. One type of commitment is periodic evaluation of one's ability and gifts for supervision. For example, supervisors may enter into a self-evaluation with their mentors several times a year, or a group of supervisors may engage in a process of self-evaluation with one another. Questions for this self-evaluation include:

> In what specific ways am I fostering a contemplative atmosphere during supervision sessions? How aware of God am I during the sessions?

> How am I helping my supervisees to develop a contemplative mind and heart and to nurture a contemplative and discerning approach to spiritual direction?

> In what ways have I kept the focus on the supervisees' inner experiences rather than the spiritual supervisors' experience?

In what ways have I failed to do so? What happens in me when I lose sight of their experience? How can I help myself to stay focused on supervisees' interior experience?

> How well am I using the supervision skills of discernment? Evocative and contemplative listening? Helping individuals notice more about their verbal responses? Reverently exploring reactions, deeper feelings, and issues? Role-playing? Offering constructive and affirming feedback?

> In what other ways am I growing as a supervisor? How is my experiential understanding of the purposes, process, and skills of supervision deepening?

> In what specific ways are my supervisees benefiting from supervision? How do I feel about the growth and changes happening within them?

Another type of commitment that supervisors can make for their ongoing growth is periodic gatherings with other supervisors to explore their inner experience while supervising and to fine-tune supervision skills. For instance, a group of supervisors in a developmental program may meet regularly to reflect on specific supervision skills they are incorporating into their supervision sessions and to practice these skills with one another. These gatherings may unfold in several ways.

> One or two supervisors may bring a challenging supervision experience to receive supervision, that is, to explore their inner experience while supervising.

> The group might form triads that include supervisee, supervisor, and observer, and engage in a supervision session. Several participants could bring a verbatim or written description of an actual direction session to practice supervision skills in a real rather than artificial way.

> Each person might present an account of a supervision session to receive the insights, observations, and suggestions of the other supervisors (a consultation approach).

> The group may engage in an open discussion about their practice of supervision skills, responding to questions such as:

  o What am I discovering about my approach to supervision as I am engaged in a session?

○ What skills am I using and which ones would I like to use more?

○ What am I noticing about my approach and use of skills that is truly facilitating my supervisees' growth in self-awareness, inner freedom, and the ability to stay with their directees' experiences?

In sum, the commitment to enter into the ministry of supervision involves not only an initial "yes" but also constant prayer and ongoing development as a supervisor. The ongoing development can occur in a variety of ways, enabling supervisors to grow in experiential knowledge, confidence, a contemplative attitude, and specific skills. It helps them to realize more deeply the seriousness of this commitment, to experience the support of other supervisors, and to enjoy more fully the dimensions of this ministry.

As the group completed their Discernment Weekend, they felt deeply renewed personally and strongly bonded as a group of supervisors. They savored the experience of being contemplative companions for one another and enthusiastically looked forward to being caring companions for their incoming group of intern spiritual directors.

Looking Toward the Future

Deeply aware that many people are looking for training programs for supervisors, they also agreed to pay attention to the call they were each experiencing to prayerfully design a six-day educational program for supervisors, that could take place twelve months from now.

As spiritual direction continues to become a professional ministry for which individuals are skillfully educated, so too supervision must be viewed with similar seriousness and professionalism. As the future unfolds, educators of supervisors are invited to reflect upon questions such as:

❯ What guiding principles are necessary for the development of competent supervisors?

❯ Is there a need for certain standards or criteria which qualify someone to be a supervisor of spiritual directors, including areas such as:

○ a proposed number of years of experience as a spiritual director,

○ a designated number of hours of experience in individual and peer group supervision,

○ an adequate background in psychology, spirituality, and group process,

○ engagement in a formal discernment process concerning one's call to the ministry of supervision,

○ education in the approach to and skills of supervision of spiritual directors,

○ commitment to working with a mentor during one's growth as a supervisor.

❯ Is there a need to develop not only workshops on supervision but also formal preparation programs for supervisors which result in receiving a Certificate or Degree in Supervision?

Conclusion

The call to the ministry of supervision is both a gift and a responsibility. As a gift, supervisors experience the awesome privilege of walking with spiritual directors in moments of struggle and joy, darkness and light, dying and rising. They are entrusted with the vulnerability and counter-pulls of their inner lives, and they facilitate the presence of God coming alive in their ministry. Supervisors are wounded healers journeying with other wounded healers in this sacred ministry of companioning others.

The call to supervision is also a responsibility because it requires a growing competency and strong commitment. Supervisors must have the educational background, experience, and skills to facilitate spiritual directors' growth in contemplation, inner awareness, and the varied gifts needed for the ministry of spiritual direction. They also need to have a deep sense of commitment to their own ongoing growth as supervisors.

"What you have received as gift give as a gift" (Mt 10:8, NAB). May we allow the manifold gifts that God has abundantly blessed us with in the ministry of spiritual direction to overflow into this growing ministry of supervision.

Bibliography

Barry, William A. "Supervision Improves Ministry." *Human Development.* 9, 1 (Spring 1988): 27–30.

Barry, William A., and William J. Connolly. *The Practice of Spiritual Direction.* New York: Seabury Press, 1982.

Birmingham, Madeline, and William J. Connolly. *Witnessing to the Fire: Spiritual Directors and the Development of Directors.* Kansas City, MO: Sheed and Ward, 1994.

Conroy, Maureen. *The Discerning Heart: Discovering a Personal God.* Chicago: Loyola Press, 1993.

Conroy, Maureen, *Looking into the Well: Supervision of Spiritual Directors.* Chicago: Loyola Press, 1995.

Estadt, Barry, John Copton, and Melvin Blanchette, eds. *The Art of Clinical Supervision: A Pastoral Counseling Perspective.* Mahwah, NJ: Paulist Press, 1987.

CHAPTER

7

∾

Immunity to Change:

Supervision, Organizational Leadership, and Transformation[1]

∾ *Margaret Benefiel* ∾

When Jean Quinn began working with the homeless population in Dublin, she found herself challenged beyond her abilities: "I was actually very frightened; I was terrified of the people. I found it hard working with the people and their behavior. I didn't much like the people. So I thought, "Well, I'm not suitable to this work."[2]

Jean, a Daughter of Wisdom, had felt drawn to work with homeless people during a sabbatical from her nursing work, when she moved to Dublin to study theology. It was the first time that she had seen people living on the streets and realized that so much homelessness existed right in her home country of Ireland.

Jean plunged into working with Dublin's homeless population and soon found herself in over her head. She realized she didn't have all the skills for dealing with issues she faced in the people she encountered, such as addiction and abuse. More importantly, she realized that her own unresolved fears and issues blocked her from serving her clients well. She knew that she would need to change if she were to continue this work.

Studies show that only one in seven individuals succeed in making a desired change even when it's a matter of life or death.[3] People in the helping professions like Jean, plunged into working with challenging people, often find they lack both the inner and outer resources to continue. Although they want to change and develop the needed capacity to meet people where they are, many people don't, and they burn out and quit.

In the terminology of Robert Kegan and Lisa Laskow Lahey, all of us carry within ourselves a strong "immunity to change."[4] Kegan and Lahey explain how we possess mental immune systems in tandem with our biological immune systems. A biological immune system serves its host well most of the time. A complex system, the immune system protects from such invaders as germs and viruses. At the same time, occasionally the immune system gets in the way of what its host needs and it can threaten its host's survival. For example, the life of an organ transplant recipient is threatened by the immune system when the immune system tries to reject the organ, which it recognizes as a foreign object.

Like our biological immune systems, our mental immune systems serve us well much of the time, protecting us from thinking and acting in ways that could endanger us. Our mental immune systems develop to ward off threats, perceived or real, and they function well at warding off those threats that stimulated their development. At the same time, our mental immune systems threaten our development when they identify a necessary change in mindset or behavior as a threat and marshal their forces to prevent that change from occurring. Our mental immune systems may even threaten our careers, our marriages, or our lives, when the changes we desire are essential to growth in any of those arenas.

Kegan and Lahey focus on how we can surface awareness of our immune systems and then, through designing safe, modest tests, challenge the assumptions that lie behind them and hold us hostage to them. Kegan and Lahey advocate working with a coach or partner in the process. This chapter focuses on how supervision can serve the same functions that Kegan and Lahey accomplish in workshops and with coaching.

With this understanding of how we all carry mental immunity to change, let's return to Jean Quinn's story.

Jean Quinn beat the odds. She changed. But it took time. On the one hand, she sought training to help her address areas with which she was unfamiliar, such as addiction. On the other hand, to look within and explore her own issues and her immunity to change, she sought supervision. Fortunately, Jean found a supervisor who was able to go deep with her, someone who brought mind, heart, and soul to supervision and helped Jean do the same in her own inner explorations. Through supervision, Jean discovered her own immunity to change, those habits and patterns she had developed that served her well at one time, in certain situations, but now were no longer serving her well. In the course of meeting with her supervisor, Jean found that, while she was working with homeless people, she was herself homeless: "I discovered I was so out of home myself, realizing that I had issues that were never addressed in my life, and discovering a whole new world."

Through working with her supervisor, Jean overcame her immunity to change and experienced transformation. Released from the inner blocks that had impeded her, Jean found new freedom and energy to address the challenges she encountered. She found herself more effective in working with her clients, able to be present to them and to help them get what they needed to address their problems.

Supervision, as Jean Quinn discovered, can help those in the helping professions overcome their immunity to change and become more effective in their work.

Immunity to change, unfortunately, isn't something that we overcome once and for all. New clients, new roles at work, and changes in life circumstances are but a few of the things that can unearth new immunities to change. Once one immunity to change is overcome, we are likely to discover another soon thereafter. One situation that invariably surfaces new immunities to change is a promotion to a leadership role.

Organizational Leadership

Individuals who become organizational leaders carry their unresolved issues into their leadership roles. In the helping professions, people who are good social workers, psychotherapists, or teachers (to name a few), get promoted to managerial and leadership positions because they are good at their original jobs, often with little or no training in leadership. In their new roles, these persons struggle to learn leadership skills on the job, all the while projecting their issues onto their teams. As Parker Palmer notes, "A leader is someone with the power to project either shadow or light onto some part of the world and onto the lives of the people who dwell there."[5] Under such conditions, it is a wonder (and a tribute to the indomitable human spirit) that organizations get anything done, let alone achieve a semblance of collegiality. Supervision can help organizational leaders come to terms with their shadows so that they can project more and more light onto their part of the world. Let's return to the story of Jean Quinn, following her as she became an organizational leader and continued her journey in supervision.

*After years of working with homeless populations, Jean noticed a pattern:
six months after finding housing for someone, she would see that person
back on the streets. Realizing that people found themselves homeless again
because their core issues hadn't been addressed, she began to wonder what
a more holistic approach to homelessness would look like. Was it possible to
attend to the deepest needs of the people she was serving as well as to their
physical needs? As Jean considered this vicious cycle, she discovered immunity
to change not only in the homeless populations, but also in the organizations
serving the homeless. Why did these organizations keep doing the same
things when they knew they were only achieving temporary fixes? Could
organizations serving homeless populations change to become more effective?
Was organizational transformation possible?*

*Over time, Jean began to dream about founding an organization with a
more holistic approach to homelessness. Could she start a new organization
that would 1) serve the homeless population in new and transformative
ways and 2) itself be open to change, renewing itself in fresh structures and
processes as needed to serve its mission? How could the supervision she had
experienced as being so important personally and professionally be integrated
into the organization?*

*In 1997, the Sophia Housing Association was born. With a mission to
"work alongside people outside of home in a holistic way," Sophia Housing
"support[s] marginalized, vulnerable and disadvantaged women, men and
children to become independent through a weaving of programs that will
provide support, education and advocacy for them."*

*As she assumed a new position as co-executive director of Sophia Housing
(with colleague Eamonn Martin as the other co-executive director), Jean
continued her supervision journey, seeking out a new supervisor, outside the
organization, for her new role, someone with organizational experience as
well as psychological training and a deep spirituality. Jean wanted to be able
to shed light on her part of the world.*

*Jean has found that, as an organizational leader, supervision helps her "look
at what's going on for me in my journey, in working with teams and individuals.
It's a way of being accountable and a place to explore what is happening in my
life, so that I'm able to separate my issues from other people's issues."*

*Furthermore, Jean and Eamonn have ensured that all the staff at Sophia
Housing have supervision, some from outside the organization and some*

from within, so that the leadership provided by the staff will be all that it can be in the organization.

Supervision can help organizational leaders encounter their shadows so that the people who dwell in their organizations can experience more light.

Organizational Change

Even an organization that is founded on holistic principles runs into problems. Organizational dysfunctionalities creep into even those organizations that are founded with the best of intentions.

Furthermore, as Michael Carroll points out, the power of the hidden "psychological contract" that humans create in their relationships contributes more complexity in organizations than it does in a relationship between two individuals.[6] Carroll explains that, in addition to the explicit business contract that humans make in their work, people also make an implicit psychological contract that only surfaces when it is violated. For example, a person may work long hours at his job, neglecting his family, in the belief that such service to the organization will assure that he will never get laid off. It is only when he is laid off and feels betrayed and angry that the psychological contract is made explicit.

As Carroll notes, psychological contracts can wreak havoc in organizations, where many layers of complexity exist. A social worker may create a psychological contract with her boss that her boss will meet her needs for support and affirmation, and with her clients that they will fulfil her need to feel like she is contributing something worthwhile to the world, all unbeknownst to the boss and the clients. Meanwhile, her boss has her own psychological contract with the social worker, and with the social worker's clients. When the psychological contracts of the social worker's team members are added to the mix, the complexity increases exponentially. Psychological contracts, until they are surfaced, create emotional undercurrents and unresolved conflicts, contributing to immunity to change.

How can organizational change occur when it is needed? How do psychological contracts get addressed in the process? What role does supervision play? Let's return to the example of Sophia Housing.

Several years into its life as an organization, Sophia Housing hit some bumps and Jean and Eamonn realized it needed to change its leadership culture. While Sophia was doing well at serving its clients holistically— honoring body, mind, and soul—internally, leadership practices from the outside world had crept in, and the holistic culture wasn't being lived out fully in the way that people within the organization related to one another. Specifically, "command and control"[7] leadership styles picked up elsewhere were working against the holistic, person-centered culture that Jean and Eamonn wanted to foster.

Seventy percent of organizational change efforts fail. Organizational leaders and organizations themselves exhibit strong immunity to change. As Kegan and Lahey note, individuals within an organization can easily fall into reinforcing one another's patterns and developing ways of being together that don't serve the goals of the organization well.[8] For example, in one team, members might admit, "We don't handle conflict well. We avoid it, and then resentments build. Plus, we don't get the benefit of differing points of view when we work on a project. The few loudest voices get their way. We have tried to change but we keep falling back into our old patterns." Or a department might discover that its immunity to change lies in its inability to assess the results of its work. It keeps doing the same things but has no idea what impact its work is having on the people it serves.

Organizational immunity to change can be harder to identify and address than individual immunity to change because of the collusion factor. Individuals get feedback regularly from their colleagues (unless something has gone seriously awry in an organization) about ways in which they need to change. Groups, on the other hand, because the members of the group are colluding in the problem, are less likely to notice and name the problem. Organizational behaviors that don't serve the organization well easily become entrenched.[9]

With these problems in mind, organizational supervision expert Sue Copeland argues that organizational leaders need to be open to what supervisors within their organizations have to offer the organization as a whole.[10] All too often, Copeland notes, supervisors are hired to work with individuals and individuals only. For example, an organization serving victims of domestic violence may hire supervisors to work with its counselors and social workers to help them become more effective in serving their clients. This is good and important work. At the same time, Copeland maintains, supervisors are in a unique position to observe, with an outsider's perspective, what is and isn't working in an organization. Supervisors note the often unintended consequences that organizational policies and procedures have on people. Supervisors see how the challenges faced by an organization impact employees. Copeland argues that supervisors should supervise "upstream" in organizations, giving feedback to organizational leaders, as well as supervising "downstream," working with direct service personnel.

Michael Carroll, like Copeland, argues that organizations desperately need supervision:

> *Organisations are amazing places to work: they are full of idealism and despair, they desperately seek change and they hate change, they create health and support amazing regression, they ask for feedback and kill when they are told what they do not want to hear, they are filled with great co-operation and incredible collusion. They are never dull. And they need supervision—badly.*[11]

Going even further than Copeland, Carroll maintains that supervisors are the best people to help organizations, better than consultants, occupational psychologists, and human resources personnel. Carroll believes that the training supervisors receive, coupled with their generally being on the margins of organizations, equips them with a "repertoire of skills, competencies, knowledge, and experience" that better positions them to address organizational issues.

How did Sophia Housing address its need for organizational change? What part did supervisors play?

Sophia Housing had identified its need for change primarily through its supervisors. Supervisors had heard about leadership practices that weren't consistent with Sophia's culture, and had supervised "upstream," gaining Jean Quinn's ear. Hidden psychological contracts surfaced when differing assumptions about leadership clashed with one another.

Once again, Sophia Housing beat the odds and effectively brought about organizational change. This time, under Jean's leadership, supervisors worked in tandem with an organizational consultant who specialized in leadership training. The organizational consultant, invited to offer leadership training in modules over six months, worked closely with supervisors, helping leaders in the organization surface their patterns, noting how leadership practices out of alignment with Sophia's culture had crept in and how everyone had colluded in not challenging them. The supervisors worked with leaders both during the program and after, continuing with them in ongoing supervision after the six months were over. Through the integration of the training and supervision, Sophia's leadership culture shifted, once again becoming more person-centered. Jean Quinn observed that, through surfacing assumptions and helping people talk about them openly, a culture of openness was created: "There's an honesty around, and there's acceptance."

Supervision can play an important role in organizational change: first, by pointing out the change that is needed; second, by surfacing hidden assumptions; and third, by serving to help bring about the change.

Conclusion

Supervisors in private practice working with individual counselors, chaplains, social workers, ministers, teachers, and spiritual directors delight in the transformations they see. Individual supervision with practitioners in the helping professions often proves more satisfying than work in organizations for several reasons. First, the individuals who seek out a supervisor in private practice often do so out of personal motivation, and so are more likely to be open to change than are individuals in the general population. Second, those in the helping professions, and especially those who are motivated to seek supervision, usually already have highly developed skills of self-reflection. Third, those in the helping professions who seek supervision have often had positive experiences of transformation through supervision in their training programs or other supervision experiences, and they are eager for more of the same. They view change and growth as desirable (unlike many people who have never tasted the power of positive transformation).

Organizational settings, for all of the reasons outlined in this chapter, often prove to be more challenging for supervisors to work in. Because of this, supervisors tend to see working with individuals in private practice as more appealing than working in organizational settings. Yet organizations desperately need what supervisors have to offer, and supervisors, as seen in the case of Sophia Housing, can make important contributions to organizations.

In organizations, immunity to change holds a grip on both the individuals who comprise it and on its teams, departments, and ultimately on the organization as a whole. Through helping individuals, teams, and the organization as a whole, supervisors can help effect individual and organizational transformation by surfacing their immunities to change and working to identify and transform the assumptions that support those immunities. May more supervisors catch a vision for what supervision can contribute to organizations, and joyfully rise to the challenge. Our organizations are crying out for what supervisors have to offer.

Notes

[1] The title of this chapter is taken from the title of the book by Robert Kegan and Lisa Laskow Lahey whose content frames this chapter: *Immunity to Change: How to Overcome it and Unlock the Potential in Yourself and Your Organization* (Boston: Harvard Business Press, 2009).

[2] The story of Jean Quinn and Sophia Housing (http://www.sophia.ie/) is the story of an actual leader and organization. She has given her permission to be quoted and for her story to be used here.

[3] Kegan and Lahey, *Immunity to Change*, 1.

[4] Ibid.

[5] P. J. Palmer, *Let Your Life Speak: Listening for the Voice of Vocation* (San Francisco: Jossey-Bass, 1999), 78.

[6] M. Carroll, "The Psychological Contract" in R. Tribe and J. Morrissey, eds., *Handbook of Professional and Ethical Practice for Psychologists, Counsellors, and Psychotherapists* (Hove: Brunner-Routledge, 2005).

[7] A "command and control" leadership style operates from a stance of "power over" employees, enforcing the leader's way, rather than drawing out employees to help them be their best selves.

[8] Kegan and Lahey, *Immunity to Change*, chapters 4 and 11.

[9] As with individual immunity to change, Kegan and Lahey advocate a workshop and coaching approach to identifying and overcoming organizational immunity to change (See, in particular, *Immunity to Change*, chapters 4 and 11). This section will examine how supervision can serve the same functions.

[10] S. Copeland, *Counselling Supervision in Organisations* (London: Routledge, 2005).

[11] M. Carroll, "Supervision in Organizations" in M. Carroll and M. Tholstrup, eds., *Integrative Approaches to Supervision* (London: Jessica Kingsley Publishers, 2001), 63.

PART II

Theories, Models, and Frameworks

CHAPTER

8

~

Dialogue and Theory in Clinical Supervision

❧ *Jack Finnegan* ☙

M*y work with postgraduate students and practitioners in applied spirituality and supervisory practice brings me into regular contact with a range of learning challenges, especially in the areas of spirituality, spiritual direction, and cross-professional supervision. Recently, while working with a group of trainee supervisors in a cross-cultural context, I found myself challenged once again by the need to come to terms not only with the reality of differing learning styles and defensive forms of working, but with the way supervisory models and styles manifest themselves in differing spaces and languages, not least in terms of the core influence of clinical supervision theory. What struck me was not only the need for a mindful metaposition and a commitment to reflection-in-action in the group I was working with, but of a misunderstanding of supervision itself as a narrow form of expert consultancy rather than a professional learning alliance with clear transformative goals. The experience brought several other factors into focus, including a poor understanding of narrative and dialogue, problems with critical self-reflection on working assumptions, and a questionable commitment to continuing professional transformation. What follows is my effort to give solid theoretical ground to my understanding of these critical and universal challenges facing contemporary supervisory practice.*

Definitions and Models

The absence of a universally agreed definition of supervision should come as no great surprise. The specialist literature is replete with an array of sometimes conflicting conceptualizations and approaches. It appears as if each author, indeed each supervisor, favors his or her own style, styles that span a spectrum from the permissive to the didactic. Permissive styles tend to cause anxiety in supervisees while didactic styles tend to generate friction between supervisor and supervisee. The challenge is to find a creative balance between the two forms of working.

Nevertheless the definitional problem does demand attention, even if the search must begin with a series of negative statements. Clinical supervision is not another form of psychotherapy, counseling, or social work. It is not another form of pastoral ministry, chaplaincy, or spiritual mentoring. Still less is it a form of directive management, individual performance review, or some other form of periodic administrative appraisal.

Definitions lie behind the models and methods to which they give rise, and in this regard there is a veritable embarrassment of riches. The history of supervision is marked by a broad confluence of approaches, all of which have impacted on the definitional problem. Definitions come from medical, clinical, social work, psychodynamic, pastoral, behavioral health, spiritual, life coaching, addiction, and family-systems sources. The development of blended models, movements towards theory integration, the identification of the generic tasks of supervision, the evolution of generic integrative models, the growth in the numbers of practitioners, the developing professionalism of the helping arts, and increasing regulation have all played their part in shaping present understandings.

Out of this confluence, a wide variety of models of supervision have been proposed. Models have been listed, systematized, and critiqued by a variety of authors including Bernard and Goodyear, Carroll, Haynes, Corey and Moulton, Gilbert and Evans, Hess, Leddick and Bernard, Powell and Brodsky, van Ooijen, and others. They include psychoanalytic and psychodynamic models, counseling models, contemplative models, developmental models, social role models, experiential-didactic models, skills and task-oriented models, family therapy models, blended models, integrative reflective and relational models, as well as models specific to supervision. Also included are alliance and relational, theory-specific, cross-professional, process, reflective, discrimination, and generic integrative models. Generic models have arisen in response to the criticism that orientation-specific models offer too narrow a base for the emerging tasks of supervision.

While models and their grounding definitions vary, they tend to encompass aspects of personal and professional support, and educational and quality assurance functions. This follows Proctor's work, which identified *restorative, formative* and *normative* elements in supervision,[1] mirroring earlier work by Kadushin who termed these elements *supportive, educational,* and *administrative-managerial* functions.[2] Systematizations that highlight the relational alliance and its core functions and constituents also influence attempts to define and describe supervision in action. However, Yegdich argues that some systematizations sidestep debate on the essential differences between supervision and therapy.[3] This is a serious question for trainee supervisors to consider because it goes to the heart of understanding the supervisor's role.

Models perform a variety of useful functions. They focus attention on a range of themes, methods, and issues:

> the functions and tasks of supervision (Kadushin; Proctor; Carroll), theoretical approaches (Jacobs),

> development issues (Stoltenberg and Delworth),

> supervisor and supervisee roles (Zalcman and Cornell),

> the process and its dynamics (Hawkins and Shohet),

> the organization of supervision (Page and Woskett),

> the supervisory context (Carroll and Holloway),

> the supervisory relationship (Feasey),

> issues of oppression (Gilbert and Evans),

> and the questions posed by blended approaches (Powell and Brodsky).

Unfortunately, the range of models does little to bring the definitional problem closer to resolution.

What Is a Model?

Models are ways of understanding complex realities. Good models share something of the quality of fine poetry. They set a tone and identify something striking about the complex and largely indefinable nature of the reality we call clinical supervision. Words and rhythms, images and expressions, meanings that are now nuanced, now replete with common sense, the humorous, the predictable, and the unexpected are juxtaposed in ways that coinvolve the partners in a dance of dialogue. They draw the partners into the bright and dark places of the human story, to the warm hearth welcoming and the boundary places scarred by forces of oppression and domination. They create a space in which understanding can come alive and play with a purpose that is at once symbolically spontaneous yet pregnant with focused possibility. Borrowing an image from Gerard Manley Hopkins, good models, like great poems, make *selving* possible.[4]

The defining quality of a good model lies in its comprehensive nature.[5] A model is a metaphor or symbol or pattern or scheme or system or structure or image or map that identifies and describes classes of activity with their tasks and processes. It is built around a pivotal concept, theoretical position, organizing image, or value and has clear cognitive, affective, and conative or active characteristics. Efficient models have informational, heuristic, interpretative, explanatory, orientating, descriptive, referential, relational, competency-based, and prognosticating capability. They will also identify optimal resources, parameters, values, objectives, constraints, and related evaluative processes. In Paul Ricoeur's terms, models give rise to thought by surfacing possibilities and their relevant theoretical and practical associations.[6]

Ian Barbour identified four principal uses of the term *model*: experimental, logical, mathematical, and theoretical.[7] Clearly, models in supervision tend to belong in the theoretical category. Barbour presents such models as "representations of selected aspects of the behavior of a complex system for particular purposes."[8] A model is an artificial construct not to be taken literally: models are not real life. They are representations, not perfect depictions, because the human situation is always in motion; its contexts are ever changing and the particularities of context are themselves in dynamic flow.

Catching hold of the human situation is at best an imprecise art. It is easy to miss what is truly happening, especially when a supervisor confuses the map with the terrain. That is another reason why a grounding in narrative and dialogue theory is so important to good supervision. Category errors occur when a theory is confused with real life, or when writing about supervision is confused with the actual practice, even if both stay near to experience as good theory or good writing must do. Yet models are more than fictions. They disclose realities despite their being unable to grasp the whole of a contextually dynamic situation in the totality of its mysteriousness. Models always call for an attitude grounded in critical realism and the practice of critical reflection.

We may not know the whole story, but what we know is truly known because good models—especially when they are used with the skilled awareness of a supervisor who has developed a conscious metaposition that observes, recognises, and understands what she or he is doing and saying—provide access to an authentic knowledge of reality in all its complexity and variety. Such knowledge may be incomplete but it is not reducible to mere subjectivity.

It was while discussing models that I chose to address narrative theory in my recent intercultural teaching experience. Narrative theory holds that people, on the basis of lived experience, create a story or script that becomes their life, the lens through which they make sense of their place in the cosmos. The supervisory relationship is intended to contribute to the healthy unfolding of two stories: that of the supervisee and that of the supervisee's client, one largely professional, the other more personal. The challenge is to support the emergence of a congruent narrative, grounded in lived experience, which opens doors to professional transformation for the supervisee, the trainee supervisor, and the well-being of the supervisee's client. In intercultural supervision the supervisor must grapple with the possible interweaving of three cultural narratives: that of the supervisor, that of the supervisee, and that of the client, especially if each comes from a different ethnic, linguistic, or gender background. The issue of interacting assumptions, presuppositions, biases, habits of mind, and expectations inevitably arises. The ethical practice of supervision requires that such intercultural interactions be critically addressed in a collaborative environment.

Models may also be described as exclusive or complementary, systematic or descriptive. Models that are exclusive or systematic are normally theory-specific or orientation-specific; they represent a worldview or paradigm with precise ways of understanding and interpreting reality. Models that are complementary or descriptive are more inclusive; they are more tentative and open-ended and are favoured in cross-theoretical and cross-professional contexts. They are humbler, alert to the fact that different models have the capacity to bring different aspects of reality and experience to light.[9]

Both forms are encountered in the context of supervision. My own intuition is to favor the humbler position precisely because any model may be complemented by the use of others. This quality is the basis for generic, integrative, and blended models. The flexibility to work with a variety of models, even when a specific model grounds and characterizes an individual supervisor's style and philosophy, seems to be a necessity for many supervisors today especially in postmodern, multicultural, and gendered contexts.

The inclusive use of integrative or blended models is responsive to the contextuality and dynamism of lived experience in a cultural milieu shaped by historical, political, educational, economic, religious, familial, local, oppressive, and liberational-developmental forces. A collaborative dialogue lies at the heart of supervision, a dialogue between persons who bear stories and culture in their own right, co-creators of meaning, actors and agents in a drama of change seeking understanding and discernment. At the very least, then, supervisors need to recognise the difference between directive, facilitative, reflective, and constructive forms of dialogue on the one hand and cultural dialogue on the other, especially in intercultural contexts.

Supervision helps to articulate and deepen understanding of this complex drama; it seeks to open important windows into its soul, to help it lean towards liberating directions. However, this capacity is dependent for the most part on the subtlety and accuracy of the philosophical, form-descriptive, and contextual presuppositions that ground a model and give rise to its insights and transformative potential.[10] Clinical supervision is always a work in progress because the drama of life continues to unfold. Supervision is not concerned with the production of final answers. It is always a journey of learning, a quest for understanding, a search for best practice and client care, and it always implies an engagement with the challenge of otherness.

The Question of Style

Style is cognate to the use of models in supervision. According to Munson, the concept of style tends to be used indiscriminately in the literature.[11] Munson develops an understanding of style by distinguishing first between active and reactive styles and then between the philosophical, theoretical, and technical styles to which the former lead. Further distinctions between structural and procedural styles, conscious and unconscious styles (non-verbal signals are typical examples), and impulsive and reflective styles are also drawn. Supervisee reactions to supervision styles are also noted. To these may be added five cognitive styles: synthesist, idealist, pragmatist, analyst, and realist.[12] Part of the difficulty is that supervisors face an embarrassment of riches when it comes to model and style choice as they develop and evolve their own styles and philosophies of supervision.

Models and styles need to be assessed not only in terms of general applicability across a range of cross-professional and intercultural contexts but also—and especially—in terms of bias, regardless of whether bias is grounded in discipline- or theory-specific questions, in uncritical enthusiasm, or in unrecognised cultural or religious beliefs. Regardless of the model chosen it is hard to see how power and gender biases, for example, can be totally eliminated. Institutionalized practices are additional contenders for critical analysis. Related themes in the *knowledge-process-skill* triad within a specific model and its role in generating images of *professional/discipline/art* identity and development also need to be critically explored.

Intercultural, linguistic, ethnic, and religious considerations also invite critical self-reflection on personal and professional assumptions and their often unconscious impact on both supervisor-supervisee and supervisee-client relationships and interactions. Problems concerning client pathogenesis are a case in point, as are prevailing assumptions that approaches to interpersonal work by atheists and agnostics are less value- or affect-laden than those of religious believers. This particular reductive bias is easy to identify in many counselor and psychotherapy trainings as well as in supervisory practice.

A similar discernible defensiveness against and reluctance to engage with ethical or moral issues is also problematic in some therapeutic approaches. The impact and validity of assumptions in these areas demand critical reflection and research. The ethical qualities—or lack thereof—of a model or style remain relevant. Boundary violations in supervision not only raise serious questions about the uses and abuses of power, rank, privilege, and status; they also raise serious ethical questions and issues of justice. It is worth recalling here that mainstreams tend to marginalize those who do not fit their prevailing models. Gender biases do not disappear because a specific style or model is in use. Nor do ethnic, religious, or cultural biases. Here is another reason why experienced supervisors give serious consideration to critical incidents and moments of difference in supervisor-supervisee and supervisee-client interactions.

Formulations of problems by supervisees present similar difficulties and challenges. The alert supervisor knows that the formulation itself may hide a range of unacknowledged assumptions, biases, prejudices, perceptions, expectations, and their related habits of mind. Regardless of the style or model in use, issues that derive from the complexity of the supervisory relationship itself arise, including anxieties, resistances, expectations, idealizations, dependencies, knowledge and skill differences, power gradients, as well as ethnic, cultural, educational, and gender differences. These and many other cognate difficulties demand integrity within the supervisory alliance if they are to be prudently and honestly identified and confronted. Against this background it is easy to understand why models and theories of gendered, ethnic, religious, and racial identity need to be studied, appreciated, and understood in the supervisory milieu.

The Metaphor of Space

The supervisory space arose as a challenging concept in my recent intercultural experience even though a significant number of authors devote time to exploring its nature. These include Carroll and Tholstrup, Foskett and Lyall, Hawkins and Shohet, Shipton, and Ward.[13] These authors tend to ground their thinking about the supervisory space in D.W. Winnicott's object relations work, especially his *Playing and Reality*.[14] In this book Winnicott identified two concepts helpful to a theoretical reflection on the kind of space conducive to creative risk taking and play inherent in supervision when it is understood as a learning alliance. The first concept is his *facilitating environment*; the second is his *potential space*. The supervisor's task, metaphorically understood in the light of Winnicott's analysis of the relationship between the child and the "good enough" parent, is the construction of a *facilitating environment* in which transformational learning and professional growth can take place. In supervision what is specifically in question is the supervisor's capacity to hold appropriate boundaries and "take responsibility for the creative possibilities and safety of the space."[15] The supervisory context is also understood as a *potential space*. This names the relational quality of the space that qualifies and characterizes the learning alliance with its responsibilities and orientations. This *potential space* names an alliance that generates the experiences that lead to trust and in so doing generates a space for creative learning and growth. It names an environment conducive to transformational learning, a safe space in which a supervisee is supported in engaging creatively and experimentally in critical self-reflection on professional engagements and the assumptions, biases, and expectations which undergird them.

Winnicott's theory allows supervisory practice to be described as a playful, imaginative, and exploratory interplay that takes place in a trusting, supportive learning alliance characterized by a creative and dynamic tension that tends towards growth and transformation. It is a safe, boundaried space for exploring states, dilemmas, paradoxes, practices, theories, incidents, problems, difficulties, challenges, relationships, suffering, pain, tragedy, joy, surprise, and wonder. Such a list is indeterminate by its nature, but exquisitely human, and even spiritual, in the dramas that lurk beneath its every nuance, its every twist and turn.

Such a view of supervision also reveals the supervisor's role as that of an educational facilitator holding a space defined by adult learning and professional purpose. This is a flexible role capable of simultaneously holding uncertainty and recognizing the need for exploration. But it is also a role that has a watching component, concerned to ensure that the exploration, its modes of action and experimentation, do no harm to the client. It is intentionally focused on reflective practice and the emergence of the critically reflective practitioner.[16] A contemplative mind has lost its rigidities. It has become open, fluid and flexible, capable of embracing the real and the transformative.

Supervision emerges here as a place to play and explore on the one hand, as a place to assess and evaluate on the other, and as a place to reflect equally and seriously on such themes as success and failure, openness and defensiveness, contemplative or empathic listening, and vulnerability. It also offers a safe space to explore the oppositional forces of exclusion and embrace, clarity and confusion, power and powerlessness, identity and otherness, struggle and obscurity, unknowing and insightful ease, as they inevitably surface in professional (and personal) relationships.

It is in such ways that transformational learning evolves, unfolds, and reveals the grounds for parallel process and other collusions, resistances, and avoidances. In Winnicott's terms, "good enough" supervision confronts all of these forces and more, becomes open to them, engages with them, dances and plays with them, and brings them to a place of potential integration. In learning to hold the dynamic tension that exists between these forces, supervision finds a source of creativity and transforming reconciliation.

The theologically informed supervisor will recognize here the spirituality implicit in supervisory practice, the traces and hints of Spirit and the Divine *perichoresis* (dance) implicit in the search for depth, meaning, for evocative encounter, and the challenge to transcend the rigidly restrictive solipsisms of defensive self-interest and the unrecognised but nevertheless destructive dynamics of narcissistic self-involvements that exclude otherness of any kind. While supervision may be described as a space for play, it is a form of play that eventually surfaces the demands of ethical responsibility for the quality of an interweaving series of human relationships. Some of these relationships engage with interiority, while others engage with external locations and the events, issues, themes, and relationships that characterize their particularities as living contexts. Such awareness is particularly relevant in intercultural situations and relationships.

In the end, the supervisor is concerned with the particularities of context and location, with their implications for the evolving quality of supervisees' professional interactions and learning, for their blind spots and dumb spots. Such considerations confront supervisory practice with an enduring challenge because, as Michel de Certeau so memorably put it, "opaque and stubborn spaces remain."[17] So does the potential for inertia. The supervisory learning spiral must continue, the play must go on, the challenges of growth and transformation must constantly be revisited, especially if the "opaque and stubborn spaces" in intercultural dialogue are to be embraced.

The Centrality of Learning in Supervision

Supervision everywhere, but especially in intercultural contexts, requires a foundation in the theory and art of reflective and transformative learning, and the metacognitive and epistemic skills that are essential to it. These metacognitive and epistemic skills include:

> ❯ self-monitoring of thought processes,
> ❯ critical awareness of the limits of knowledge and certainty,
> ❯ and critical understanding of the criteria for knowledge.

I have found Professor Jack Mezirow's work on transformational learning to be particularly relevant in this context.[18] Supervision is tasked with creating a space where commitment to learning (the heart of continued professional development) is considered foundational to best practice and is offered continuing support. Once it is accepted that supervision implies a learning alliance, two related themes promptly arise: the need for critically reflective and transformative learning skills, and the challenge to respond creatively to different supervisee learning styles.[19]

In Sweden, where formal supervision training has been regulated for more than twenty years, Imre Szecsödy has continued to develop work that distinguishes between *cognitive styles* (to do with perceptions and characteristic modes of thinking), *working styles* (to do with selective use of fundamental concepts and theories), and *defensive styles* (to do with character traits and the interweaving of transfer and counter-transfer phenomena, sometimes referred to as movements and counter-movements is spiritual direction).[20] Szecsödy also draws attention to *accommodative learning* (new learning leads to a modification of existing cognitive schemata), and *assimilative learning* (new learning is added to old). Szecsödy's understanding of accommodative learning compares well with Mezirow's theory of transformative learning.

Accommodative or transformative learning is what is ideally sought in the supervision process. Professional supervisors and supervisors in training require the ability to identify supervisee (and client) learning styles, learning needs, learning goals, and learning challenges. These categorizations bring Kolb's experiential learning theory (he distinguishes between *activist, reflector, theorist,* and *pragmatist* learning styles) firmly into play in the supervisory relationship. Supervision is always concerned with experiential knowledge and its transformative potential as it is brought into dialogue with other (sometimes expert) opinions and experiences.[21] Personality preferences and typology also play a part here,[22] and Munson's further identification of *error acceptance learning* is particularly relevant in contexts where supervisee-learning evaluation is in play.[23]

Reflection-in-Action

The capacity for reflection-in-action became a much discussed issue in my recent intercultural experience in teaching supervisory practice. Much of a supervisor's work has to do with exploring and testing the reliability of modes of action and interpretation. Good practice requires the development of accurate professional knowledge. Professional knowledge requires critical familiarity with processes of reflection-in-action. And good supervision requires the capacity to engage in reflective and collaborative dialogue with another. It is this capacity that is the continuing object of reflection-in-action. Testing interpretations or attributions, surfacing negative reactions and judgments, and facing disorienting dilemmas are essential to developing reflection-in-action skills.[24]

Reflection-in-action involves the ability to think reflectively about thinking while engaged in thinking. It also implies the ability to hold a conscious *metaposition* during the supervisory session (a critically reflective and attentive overview of what I am thinking, feeling, doing—and why). Critical awareness of the quality and flow of one's own awareness is fundamental to a supervisor's repertoire of skills.

A good metaposition leans in the direction of alert, attentive, even contemplative awareness. There is nothing magical here. The reflective-action stance will verify how sensitively supervisors observe and grasp in context their role and the quality of their participation in the supervision process. The development of a reflective metaposition not only generates perspective and breadth of vision, it recognizes the dance of alternatives in a many-voiced network of positions, and within the constraints of time that enables them all to emerge and play their part.[25]

A good metaposition allows the supervisor to watch the process, to clarify, and to give accurate feedback about its modes of communication, its narratives and interpretations, and its impacts and conclusions. It will surface such themes as lack and conflict, interactive frame and boundary difficulties, individual hot spots and fault lines, blind spots, deaf spots and dumb spots, and other factors that may require personal work. Clarity around two forms of frame and two forms of boundary is required: frames of interpretation and knowledge; and personal and organizational boundaries. A good supervisor also understands the interplay of time frames, frames of reference, frames of mind, and ethical and professional boundaries.

A good metaposition also permits the supervisor to bridge the gap between *discipline-oriented thinking* and *practice-oriented thinking*, a skill that is crucial to the supervisor's art. When the challenge of this gap is not recognized the result is fragmented thinking: theoretical monologues running in parallel, one trying to trump the other. Discipline-oriented thinking tends to have a narrow, reductive focus that can easily become coercive and domineering. Playful supervision requires a more interdisciplinary, fluid, contemplative, topic-oriented approach. Practice-oriented approaches focus on what unfolds between the people involved in the supervisory dialogue, the concepts and symbols that are at work, and the interpretations that arise.

When supervisors model an attentive metaposition that bridges the gap between discipline-oriented and practice-oriented thinking, they empower supervisees to take more assured and autonomous possession of their own learning and knowledge. An attentive metaposition also supports the emergence of a supervisee-led process grounded in discovery and a reverent mutuality. Ability to work with the gap between discipline-oriented thinking and practice-oriented thinking is important for another reason. Training programs must deal with it if what they do is to be professionally and academically convincing, more particularly when they take place in academic settings where the theory-practice gap engenders contested understandings of interdisciplinary study.[26]

Without well-developed metacognitive skills it is difficult to see how a supervisor can sustain the ability to monitor, clarify, and orient the theoretical and interpersonal dynamics that characterize interpersonal helping relationships, particularly in intercultural situations. The same must be said about reflection-in-action and critical self-reflection on assumptions. They are all essential to the contemporary understanding of adult experiential learning.[27] By implication supervisors and supervisees must be willing to subject both theory and practice to critical examination in a safe learning alliance that is open to critical and reflective self-questioning.

Here is one of the reasons why the good therapist, or good pastoral or spiritual practitioner, does not always make a good supervisor. The learning focus and the skill sets are quite different. A capacity for reflection-in-action and critical self-reflection on assumptions is essential for successful continuing professional development. It is especially necessary in cross-professional and intercultural supervisory contexts.

Metacognition is a quality of awareness and reflection that ensures that learning and understanding goals are identified and met during the supervisory encounter. Metacognitive signals (often non-verbal) will indicate when something has not been understood. They will specify the presence of an impasse, a resistance, an edge, a block, or a moment of difference, and will invite reflective ways to discover an avenue of approach or a solution. Metacognition supports the capacity to assess and monitor the mode of a particular understanding, interpretation, pattern, knowing, or direction. It implies a feel for what is going on; and it also involves effective use of memory and comprehension.

Metacognition has strategic value. Supervisors and practitioners who are critically reflective and metacognitively skilled are usually more confident, more likely to think through failures and problems, and more likely to seek personal help because they view themselves as life-long learners open to expanding their personal and professional repertoire of skills. Such supervisors have developed the habit of thinking about their thinking and are intentionally open to conceptual change.[28]

Bakhtin's Dialogics and Supervision

The single most significant issue to arise during my recent intercultural exchanges had to do with dialogic theory and my own preference for the theories of Mikhail Bakhtin. Considered in the context of supervisory practice, dialogic theory permits several problems to be confronted. Supervision is concerned with theoretically grounded practice and the emergence of a practical theory of relationality that permits forces and practices expressive of agency and resistance to be surfaced in the process of professional development through critical reflection on its shape and form within a range of professional and related sociocultural contexts. It is helpful here to consider Michael Holquist's definition of Bakhtinian dialogics in terms of a relationship "in which differences—while still remaining different—serve as the building blocks of simultaneity."[29]

In effect, supervisors need to remember that both resistance and agency are determined by position: who sits where in what cultural context? This is particularly relevant when factors such as race, class, gender, education, and religion affect the linguistic or narrative forms that give agency and resistance—difference—expression. At the same time it is important to note with Dale Bauer and Susan Mckinstry that "speech is not always a sign of power, or silence a sign of weakness."[30] Again, dialogue implies the presence of several voices; it is the opposite of monologue. Bakhtin's dialogics reminds supervisors and supervisees alike of the flattening dangers of the monologue, and that a whole spectrum of shaping voices is actually present in the supervisory space, voices that need to be surfaced and heard. We face an indeterminate range of coincidences and polarities as shaping voices dance in and out and all around in the supervisory dialogue.

Monologic and reductive understandings and interpretations of the issues and assumptions that arise in supervisory contexts are therefore at best inappropriate. Every expression is a social construct, a two-sided phenomenon composed by one person for another. Language is not free floating, timeless, impersonal. Supervisor and supervisee each give themselves verbal shape in the dialogue being spun between them. But more importantly each gives verbal shape to him or herself from the other's point of view. A self is woven in a dialogue that is both contingent and social in nature. It emerges in the flow of question and answer and relationality. Good supervisors recognize when they begin to reveal different faces and different voices.

Mimesis and surface performance are always potentially present: the supervisor playing one part, the supervisee the other, with the absent client as a kind of ghostly or invisible presence hinted at in the subversive presence of parallel processes.[31] The same is true of organizational and institutional presences. The supervisor's task is to be alert to these forces and to deconstruct them in such a way as to open the narrative up to further inquiry. In so doing the monologue is opened up to dialogue as new questions, unsettling questions, unexpected questions move the discourse towards dialogic responsibility precisely because there is no neutrality in discourse or narrative, no neutral definitions. What is present is the dangerous power to subsume the other, subsume difference, and spin it into a bland untroubling sameness.

Let me say it again. The supervisor does not meet the client. The supervisor meets a spoken text. The problem is that this text may readily smooth over and unify what is a scattered spectrum of differences, of social forces, themes and events, issues and dilemmas, struggles and surrenders, oppressions and marginalizations. For the alert supervisor, language is where core struggles and dramas are most comprehensively—and at the same time most intimately and most personally engaged—nowhere more so than in intercultural and interlinguistic contexts. As Katerina Clark and Michael Holquist put it, it is in language that social force finds its most realized expression because in Bakhtin's view each word "is a little arena for the clash and criss-crossing of differently oriented social accents."[32] Let us unfold social accents to include cultural, ethnic, geographic, religious, and gendered accents.

The key questions for the supervisor are: "What voice am I hearing?; Whose voice am I hearing?; What is really happening in this narration, this text?; How is it reconstructing my supervisee in the telling?; and How will it reconstruct me as I enter it in dialogue?" In this sense the supervisory relationship operates at the level of language, narrative, and textuality, and is developed there. Ultimately, it is a question of intuiting, surfacing, and rearticulating the intentions hidden in normative discourse, of recognizing the oppositional difference between inner and outer speech. This process is not easy at the best of times. How challenging it is when the social accents are heard through differing cultural media.

As Bakhtin learnt only too well in Stalinist Russia, monologues silence other voices and marginalize difference: another reason why supervisor monologues are suspect. It is not that supervision avoids silence; it is that supervision recognizes in the messiness of dialogue something of the deeper truth and mysteriousness of the human situation. In Bakhtinian terms, supervision may be described as a work that is always in process, a polyphony always awaiting completion. Understood in this way supervisory dialogues intentionally hold differences together in a web of interconnections whose extent is immeasurable. There is always more than one meaning in a story and the supervisory task is to explore as many of them as time and syntax make possible, because Bakhtinian dialogics are syntagmatic (to do with the actual relationship between words in a sequence: e.g., how do the words *the sun is shining* relate to each other?) rather than paradigmatic (to do with the substitution of words: e.g., substituting sun with stars) in their understanding of self-other interactions and differences.[33]

In effect, in the supervisory relationship—as elsewhere—existence itself confronts us with "a riot of inchoate potential messages."[34] We can either ignore these stimuli or respond to them in an effort to make sense by discriminating among their perceived values. We reduce them to manageable proportions by recognizing the ideological import of what is addressed to us and that calls us forth in self-creating responses. Why? Because life is a form of semiotic expression made up of signs, symbols, and meanings.

In the beginning was the Word. Then the word was made flesh: the self is born of the dialogic structure of consciousness itself. The self is known in the response of the other whether this other is an individual, a neighborhood, a class, a culture, or some other. It is only in discourse with the Other that the Self is defined. In terms of defining the nature of supervisory practice, the identification of this otherness and a differential dialogue with it becomes essential to clarity.

Such dialogue is especially relevant in contexts; intercultural contexts are a case in point, where competing definitions and meanings are encountered. Terminology from other discourses help. In ethnography the dialogue between emic (subjective) and etic (theoretical) conceptions of a given phenomenon, the valuing of the dialogic interaction of subjective and theoretical learning and unlearning is a useful example for the discerning supervisor concerned with understanding and elucidating the multiple meanings and social accents of any discourse. This is particularly so in terms of those elements of a supervisory conversation that are experience-near or experience-distant.

Put simply, dialogic supervision recognizes the many voices of human discourse. More importantly, it values the mutual reconstruction of the phenomenon at issue in an engaged dialogue: each speaking from his or her own egocentric and cultural position with respect to the other.[35] The particular contribution of the dialogic approach is not only to take into consideration the complexity of communication as such, but also to understand communication contextually as organically connected to the whole of life. Voices have faces.

Dialogic supervision has a major contribution to make. The uncertainties of representation, the problems associated with "hard data," the resistance to otherness and depth, the tendencies towards reductionism and the like, are all taken into consideration in the dialogic approach. The conventional approach is to consider a basic context, identify occurrences and the interpretative filters through which they are apprehended, and engage in conversation about them. The danger here is model- or theory-driven reductionism with the supervisor actually unconsciously controlling what happens.

The dialogic approach is essentially anthropological. It favors an exegetical approach to real-life dialogue and is especially interested in the actual irregularities and unpredictability of live narrative. It is aware of the necessity for at least two voices if creative awareness is to emerge. The dialogic approach maintains openness to surprise and creativity in everyday life and its descriptions. It recognizes that the past leaks into the present and leaves traces.[36] It understands that utterances take place "in already inhabited interactional zones."[37] Words and utterances are many voiced. They reveal both centrifugal and centripetal dynamics: the centripetal dynamics of the monologue with its pull towards ideological or theoretical standardization; and the centrifugal or decentralizing dynamics of empowering dialogue.

What Bakhtin's theory teaches the supervisor is that words have many layers of meaning. They reveal the influences of many different contexts. Words and utterances sit in the transitional spaces between speakers and listeners; they become encrusted with meanings flowing from one's own and others' perceptual horizons. The influence of more than one context is always at work: meanings are constantly interacting. There is always a polyphony of social and discursive forces at work, a diversity of social speech types and faces surfacing in everyday life. Networks of dialogic meanings and the interactions between multiple meanings contest the push towards unitary meanings. They surface conscious backgrounds and give rise to responses and objections. Supervisors who are not alert to dialogic complexity are at a distinct disadvantage, especially in cross-professional and intercultural supervisory contexts. The last thing supervision requires is to become mired in unconscious sets of parallel monologues, each voice seeking to make its point and win.

The power gradient in the supervisory relationship tends to arise explicitly in monologues, more particularly when appeal is made to normative or theoretical rules. What is particularly attractive about the dialogic approach is its mindful capacity to favor the persuasive word over the authoritative word in energizing genuinely transformative learning: learning grounded in internal dialogue. The core of Bakhtin's message for the supervisor is that narratives and meanings remain many voiced. They reveal many interactive influences, even when what is said is deeply personal.

Supervisors are consistently challenged to embrace narrative diversity, a process that demands critical self-reflection on assumptions with their usually unrecognized habits of mind and expectations. Supervisors are challenged to enhance the quality and depth of the supervisory conversation by making the questioning of assumptions a contextual necessity. The goal is always critical reflection and professional growth, not power or control. The problem with power and control in the supervisory relationship, as elsewhere, is that it does not circulate; it tends to accumulate, to become increasingly asymmetrical.

In this sense dialogic supervision is always alert to the issues of equality, to the call to respect deep democracy and its many voices, to be open to change in perspectives and arrival at a reasonable consensual agreement. More to the point, in the dialogical approach the process is important, not the consensus achieved or the disagreements that remain. Respect for the process implies that everything is open to scrutiny, especially those elements that surface otherness and difference in the search for understanding. The call to the supervisor is to take the dialogue as far as possible while watching for the moment when it ceases to be useful or helpful: negative feedback is recognized and respected.

In the end the dialogic approach to supervision is about recognizing the value of dialogue. It is not only concerned with coming to grips with real-life utterances, with narratives, words, or texts. The concern is at a deeper level. Dialogical supervision engages with the shaping and framing forces that are at work as supervisor and supervisee dialogically construct what are best described as complex unities of difference.[38] Even in our agreements, personal, cultural, and professional differences remain to be celebrated.

Concluding Thoughts

More than thirty years ago Ekstein and Wallerstein had already drawn attention to a fundamental danger in all models and styles of supervision. This is the danger posed by *closed system learning*, the tendency simply to add new learning to old and in the adding block meaningful change. The danger becomes more acute in intercultural contexts and situations. Closed system learning represents the propensity to reduce the new, the different, and the unfamiliar to the already known. It supports stagnation by falling back on trusted prior learning and skills, for example, the tendency to fall back on skills learnt and developed in prior therapeutic, pastoral, or spiritual training and practice, as well as unquestioned cultural assumptions—whether or not these are relevant or appropriate to the facts of the supervisory relationship and its present particularities.

The repercussions of this tendency are particularly significant for the trainee supervisor; time needs to be spent critically reflecting on the tendency's personal, cultural, and practice-oriented implications. Raising the issue of closed system learning permits me to close these reflections as I opened them, with a clear focus on transformative learning alert to intercultural challenge.

I also want to reiterate that approaches derived from models of clinical supervision are most likely to provide a safe containing environment for practitioners from other helping professions and arts. This is especially true when we are concerned with identifying appropriate cross-professional supervision models and styles for use in non-therapeutic, pastoral, or spiritual contexts. Care is needed with this suggestion, however, because in some cultural contexts clinical supervision offered in a professional key is seen as too challenging, and herein rests the potential for adverse misunderstandings and the complications they cause, especially in second-language contexts.

Spiritual and pastoral practitioners who, for defensive religious reasons, resist calls to adopt professional standards and ethics are a case in point. The result is continuing problems around boundary crossing and boundary violation. Hopefully, experience with integrative and blended models and contemplative styles of supervision will help smooth these difficulties. Good clinical supervision, after all, represents a privileged moment in life-long adult learning. It represents a potentially transformative dialogical encounter with another. More significantly, clinical supervision has the power to open portals to clearer visions and wiser, more creative, and liberating potentials for the developing professional self, especially in intercultural contexts where the very nature of clinical supervision raises important questions, not least of which are the nature of power and authority in contexts struggling with subtle neo-colonial forces. But that is another story for another time.

Notes

[1] B. Proctor,."Supervision: A Co-Operative Exercise in Accountability" in *Enabling and Ensuring* (ed. M. Markan and M Payne; Leicester: National Youth Bureau and Council for Education and Training in Youth and Community Work, 1986).

[2] The first edition of Kadushin's text was published in 1976.

[3] T. Yegdich, ."Lost in the Crucible of Supportive Clinical Supervision: Supervision is Not Therapy," *Journal of Advanced Nursing*, 29:5 (1999): 1265–75.

[4] Sonnet 34, As kingfishers catch fire. Gerard Manley Hopkins, *Gerard Manley Hopkins: The Major Works*, ed. Catherine Philips (Oxford: Oxford University Press, 2002).

[5] B. Proctor, *Group Supervision: A Guide to Creative Practice* (London: Sage, 2000).

[6] P. Ricoeur, *The Symbolism of Evil* (Boston: Beacon Press, 1967), 347–57.

[7] I. G. Barbour, *Myths, Models and Paradigms: A Comparative Study in Science and Religion* (Boston: Beacon Press, 1974), 29–30.

[8]Ibid., 6.

[9]S. B. Bevans, *Models of Contextual Theology* (Maryknoll, NY: Orbis Books, 1994), 24–26.

[10]Ibid., 55–67.

[11]C. E. Munson, *Handbook of Clinical Social Work Supervision* Third Edition (New York: Hawthorn Press, 2002), 115.

[12]Ibid., 115–48.

[13]See Michael Carroll and Margaret Tholstrup, *Integrative Approaches to Supervision* (London: Jessica Kingsley, 2001), 24; John Foskett and David Lyall, *Helping the Helpers: Supervision and Pastoral Care* (London: SPCK, 1988), 114; Peter Hawkins and Robin Shohet, *Supervision in the Helping Professions* (Buckingham: Open University Press, 2002), 3ff; Geraldine Shipton, *Supervision of Counselling and Psychotherapy: Making a Place to Think* (Buckingham: Open University Press, 1997), 73; Frances Ward, *Lifelong Learning: Theological Education and Supervision* (London: SCM Press, 2005), 88–95.

[14]D.W. Winnicott, *Playing and Reality* (London and New York: Routledge, 1999).

[15]Frances Ward, *Lifelong Learning*, 88.

[16]See Jennifer Moon, *A Handbook of Reflective and Experiential Learning: Theory and Practice* (London and New York: Routledge-Falmer, 2004).

[17]Michel de Certeau, *The Practice of Everyday Life* (Berkeley: University of California Press, 1988), 201.

[18]See J. Mezirow, "Learning to Think Like an Adult: Core Concepts of Transformation Theory" in *Learning as Transformation: Critical Perspectives on a Theory in Progress* (San Francisco: J. Mezirow and Associates, 2000), 3–33. This book should be required reading for all supervisors in training.

[19]Learning style represents a practical means of identifying learner interaction or learning approach. See D. A. Kolb, *Experiential Learning: Experience as the Source of Learning and Development* (2nd ed.; Englewood Cliffs, NJ: Prentice Hall, 1984). See also, R. R. Sims and S. J., eds., *The Importance of Learning Styles: Understanding the Implications for Learning, Course Design, and Education* (Westport, CT: Greenwood Press,1995). And G. Nicholls, *Developing Teaching and Learning in Higher Education* (London: Routledge-Falmer, 2002).

[20]I. Szecsödy, "(How) Is Learning Possible in Supervision?" in *Supervision and its Vicissitudes* (eds. B. Martindale et al.; London: H. Karnac Books Ltd., 1997), 101–16, at 106.

[21]Kolb,. op.cit.

[22]P. Cranton, "Individual Differences and Transformative Learning" in Jack Mezirow and Associates, op.cit., 181–204.

[23]C. E. Munson, *Handbook of Clinical Social Work Supervision* (3rd ed.; New York, London, Oxford: The Haworth Press, 2002), 241–42.

[24]See D. A. Schön *The Reflective Practitioner: How Professionals Think in Action* (Aldershot: Avebury, 1991), 105–67. These pages are particularly relevant to the supervisory context. See also his *Educating the Reflective Practitioner* (San Francisco: Jossey-Bass, 1986), 231–302.

[25]For an interesting discussion of this role, see J. Goodbread, *The Dreambody Toolkit: A Practical Introduction to the Philosophy, Goals and Practice of Process-Oriented Psychology* (2nd ed.; Portland, OR: Lao Tse Press, 1997), 48–49.

[26]See P. Weingart and N. Stehr, *Practising Interdisciplinarity* (Toronto, Buffalo, London: Toronto University Press, 2000); R. F. Dillon and J. W. Pellegrino, eds., *Instruction: Theoretical and Applied Perspectives* (New York & London: Praeger Publishers, 1991), 107–116; D. A. Schön, *The Reflective Practitioner* op.cit., pp. 144–145.

[27]L. A. Parks Daloz, "Transformative Learning for the Common Good" in Jack Mezirow & Associates, *Learning as Transformation*, 103–123.

[28]J. H. Flavell coined the term *metacognition* in 1976 and noted its learning-relevant properties. Concern is with intentional conceptual change. See T. J. Perfect and B. L. Schwartz, *Applied Metacognition* (Cambridge: Cambridge University Press, 2002); M. Ferrari and L. V. Shavinina, eds., *Beyond Knowledge: Extracognitive Aspects of Developing High Ability* (Mahwah, NJ: Lawrence Erlbaum Associates, 2002); D.Yun Dai and R. J. Sternberg, eds., *Motivation, Emotion, and Cognition: Integrative Perspectives on Intellectual Functioning and Development* (Mahwah, NJ: Lawrence Erlbaum Associates, 2004); P. R. Pintrich and G. M. Sinatra, eds., *Intentional Conceptual Change* (Mahwah, NJ: Lawrence Erlbaum Associates, 2003).

[29]M. Holquist, *Dialogism: Bakhtin and His World* (London: Routledge, 2002), 40.

[30]D. M. Bauer and S. J. McKinstry, "Introduction" in D. M. Bauer and S. J. McKinstry, eds., *Feminism, Bakhtin and the Dialogic* (Albany, NY: State University of New York Press, 1991).

[31]See G. M. Schwab, "Irigarayan Dialogism: Play and Powerplay" in ibid., 57–72.

[32]See K. Clark and M. Holquist, *Mikhail Bakhtin* (Cambridge, MA: Harvard University Press, 1984), 220.

[33]See Holquist, *Dialogism*, 43.

[34]Ibid., 47.

[35]Ibid.,110.

[36]Ibid., 120 , 135.

[37]Ibid., 121.

[38]See J. P. Zappen, "Mikhail Bakhtin" in *Twentieth-Century Rhetorics and Rhetoricians: Critical Studies and Sources* (ed. M. Ballif and M. G. Moran; Westport, CT: Greenwood Press, 2000), 7–22.

Select Bibliography

Adelson M. J. (1995). "Clinical Supervision of Therapists with Difficult to Treat Patients" in *Bulletin of the Menninger Clinic,* 59(1):32–52.

Alien, C. and A. Brazier. (1996). "Support for Clinical Supervisors: From Training to Play Space," *Clinical Psychology Forum* 85:37–39.

Anderson, L. W. and L. A. Sosniak, eds. (1994). *Bloom's Taxonomy: A Forty-Year Retrospective.* Chicago: University of Chicago Press.

Anderson, L. W. et al., eds. (2001). *Taxonomy of Learning for Teaching: A Revision of Bloom's Taxonomy of Educational Objectives.* New York: Addison-Wesley-Longman.

Arlow, J. A. (1963). "The Supervisory Situation," *Journal of the American Psychoanalytic Association,* 11(3):576–94.

Bandura, A. (1965). " 'Influence of Models' Reinforcement Contingencies on the Acquisition of Imitative Responses," *Journal of Personality and Social Psychology,* 1:589–95.

Barbour, I.G. (1974). *Myths, Models and Paradigms: A Comparative Study in Science and Religion.* Boston: Beacon Press.

Barnes, G.G., G. Down and D. McCann. (2000). *Systemic Supervision: A Portable Guide for Supervision Training.* London & Philadelphia: Jessica Kingsley Publishers.

Baumgartner, L. and S. B. Merriam. (2000). *Adult Learning and Development: Multicultural Stories.* Malabar, FL: Krieger Publishing.

Beinart, H. (2002). "An Exploration of Factors which Predict the Quality of the Relationship in Clinical Supervision" *D. Clin.Psych*, diss., Open University/British Psychological Society.

Bernard, J.M. and R. K.Goodyear. (2004). *Fundamentals of Clinical Supervision.* 3rd ed. Boston: Pearson A and B.

Bevans, S.B. (1994). *Models of Contextual Theology.* Maryknoll, NY: Orbis Books.

Binder, J. and H. Strupp. (1997). "Supervision of Psychodynamic Psychotherapies," in *Handbook of Psychotherapy Supervision.* Edited by C. E. Watkins Jr. New York: Wiley.

Birk, J.M. and J. R. Mahalik. (1996). "The Influence of Trainee Conceptual Level, Trainee Anxiety, and Supervision Evaluation on Counsellor Developmental Level," *The Clinical Supervisor,* 14:123–37.

Blocher, D.H. (1983). "Supervision in Counseling: Contemporary Models of Supervision: Toward a Cognitive Developmental Approach to Counseling Supervision," *Counseling Psychologist,* 11:27–34.

Bloom, B.S. et al., eds. (1956). *Taxonomy of Educational Objectives: Handbook 1: Cognitive Domain.* New York: McKay.

Bond, M. and S. Holland. (1998). *Skills of Clinical Supervision for Nurses.* Buckingham: Open University Press.

Bordin, E.S. (1983). "A Working Alliance Model of Supervision," *Counseling Psychologist,* 11:35–42.

Borgen, W.A. and R. A.Young, eds. (1990). *Methodological Approaches to the Study of Career.* New York: Praeger Publishers.

Bower, G. and E. Hilgard. (1981). *Theories of Learning*. 5th ed. Englewood Cliffs, NJ: Prentice Hall.

Bulmer, M. and J. Solomos. eds. (1999). *Ethnic and Racial Studies Today*, London: Routledge.

Burke, W.R., R. K. Goodyear and C. Guzzard. (1998). "Weakenings and Repairs in Supervisory Alliances: A Multiple-Case Study," *American Journal of Psychotherapy*, (52)4:450–62.

Carroll, M. (1996). *Counselling Supervision: Theory, Skills and Practice*. London: Cassell.

Carroll, M. (1999). "Training in the Tasks of Supervision," in *Training Counselling Supervisors*. Edited by E.L. Holloway and M. Carroll. London: Sage.

Carroll, M. and E. L. Holloway. (1996). "Reaction to the Special Section on Supervision Research: Comment on Ellis et al. (1996), Ladany et al. (1996), Neufeldt et al. (1996), and Worthen and McNeill (1996)," *Journal of Counseling Psychology*, 43:51–55.

Carroll, M. and E. L. Holloway. (1999). *Counselling Supervision in Context*. London: Sage.

Carroll, M. and M. Tholstrup. (2001). *Integrative Approaches to Supervision*. London and Philadelphia: Jessica Kingsley Publishers.

Caspi, J. and W. J. Reid. (2002). *Educational Supervision in Social Work: A Task-Centered Model for Field Instruction and Staff Development*. New York: Columbia University Press.

Corbett, L. (1995). "Supervision and the Mentor Archetype," in *Jungian Perspectives on Clinical Supervision*. Edited by P. Kugler. Switzerland: Daimon Einsiedeln.

Cranton, P. (1994). *Understanding and Promoting Transformative Learning: A Guide for Educators of Adults*. San Francisco: Jossey-Bass.

Cranton, P. (2000). "Individual Differences and Transformative Learning." Pages 181–204 in Jack Mezirow and Associates, *Learning as Transformation: Critical Perspectives on a Theory in Progress*. San Francisco: Jossey-Bass.

Culbreth, John R. and Lori L. Brown, eds. (2010). *State of the Art in Clinical Supervision*. New York and Hove: Routledge.

D'Andrea, M. and J. Daniels. (1997). "Multicultural Counseling Supervision: Central Issues, Theoretical Considerations, and Practical Strategies," in *Multicultural Counseling Competencies: Assessment, Education, Training and Supervision*. Edited by D.B. Pope-Davis and H.L.K. Coleman. Thousand Oaks, CA: Sage.

Dennis, M. (2001). "An Integrative Approach to 'Race' and Culture in Supervision," in *Integrative Approaches to Supervision*. Edited by M. Carroll and M. Tholstrup. London: Jessica Kingsley.

Dillon, R.F. and J. W. Pellegrino, eds. (1991). *Instruction: Theoretical and Applied Perspectives*. New York and London: Praeger Publishers.

Duan, C.M. and H. Roehlke. (2001). "A Descriptive 'Snapshot' of Cross-Racial Supervision in University Counseling Center Internships." *Journal of Multicultural Counseling and Development*, 29(2):131–46.

Dye, H. A. (1987). *ACES Attitudes: Supervisor Competencies and a National Certification Program*. ERIC/CAPS Resources in Education, Document No. ED 283 098. ERIC Clearinghouse on Counselling and Student Services, Greensboro, NC.

Edwards, D. (1997). "Supervision Today: The Psychoanalytic Legacy," in *Supervision of Psychotherapy and Counselling,*. Edited by G. Shipton. Buckingham: Open University Press.

Ekstein, R. and R. S.Wallerstein. (1958). *The Teaching and Learning of Psychotherapy.* New York: Basic Books.

Ekstein R. and R. S. Wallerstein. (1972). *The Teaching and Learning of Psychotherapy.* 2nd ed. New York: International Universities Press.

Elias, J.L. and S. B. Merriam. (2005). *Philosophical Foundations of Adult Education.* 3rd ed. Malabar, FL: Krieger Publishing.

Erwin, W.J. (2000). "Supervisor Moral Sensitivity." *Counselor Education and Supervision,* 40(2):115–27.

Faugier J. and T. Butterworth. (1993). *Clinical Supervision—A Position Paper.* Manchester: School of Nursing Studies, University of Manchester.

Feasey, D. (2002). *Good Practice in Supervision with Psychotherapists and Counsellors.* London: Whurr Publishers.

Ferrari, M. and L. V. Shavinina, eds. (2003). *Beyond Knowledge: Extracognitive Aspects of Developing High Ability.* Mahwah, NJ: Lawrence Erlbaum Associates.

Field, K. P. Holden, and H. Lawlor. (2000). *Effective Subject Leadership.* London & New York: Routledge.

Flavell, J. H. (1979). "Metacognition and Cognitive Monitoring: A New Area of Cognitive-Developmental Inquiry." *American Psychologist,* 34:906–11.

Flavell, J. H. (1987). "Speculations about the Nature and Development of Metacognition." Pages 21–29 in *Metacognition, Motivation and Understanding.* Edited by F. E. Weinert and R. H. Kluwe. Hillside, NJ: Lawrence Erlbaum Associates.

Fleming, I. and L. Steen, eds. (2003). *Supervision and Clinical Psychology: Theory, Practice and Perspectives.* Hove & New York: Brunner-Routledge.

Fong, M.L. et al., eds. (1997). "Becoming a Counselor: A Longitudinal Study of Student Cognitive Development." *Counselor Education and Supervision,* 37:100–14.

Fowler, J. (1996). "The Organisation of Clinical Supervision within the Nursing Profession: A Review of the Literature." *Journal of Advanced Nursing,* 23:471–78.

Fowler, J., ed. (1998). *The Handbook of Clinical Supervision: Your Questions Answered.* Salisbury, Wiltshire: Mark Allen Publishing Ltd.

Freund, A.M. and P. B. Baltes. (2000). "The Orchestration of Selection, Optimization, and Compensation: An Action Theoretical Conceptualization of a Theory of Developmental Regulation." Pages 35–58 in *Control of Human Behavior, Mental Processes, and Consciousness: Essays in Honor of the 60th Birthday of August Flammer.* Edited by A Grob and W. J. Perrig. Mahwah, NJ: Lawrence Erlbaum Associates.

Friedlander, M.L. and L. G. Ward. (1984). "Development and Validation of the Supervisory Styles Inventory." *Journal of Counseling Psychology,* 31:541–57.

Fukuyama, M.A. (1994) "Critical Incidents in Multicultural Counseling Supervision: A Phenomenological Approach to Supervision Research," *Counselor Education and Supervision,* 34:142–47.

Gilbert, M.C. and K. Evans. (2000). *Psychotherapy Supervision: An Integrative Relational Approach to Psychotherapy Supervision.* Buckingham: Open University Press.

Glanz, J. and L. S. Behar-Horenstein. (2000). *Paradigm Debates in Curriculum and Supervision: Modern and Postmodern Perspectives.* Westport, CT: Bergin & Garvey.

Goodbread, J. (1997). *The Dreambody Toolkit: A Practical Introduction to the Philosophy, Goals and Practice of Process-Oriented Psychology.* 2nd ed. Portland, OR: Lao Tse Press.

Granello, D.H., P. H. Beamish and T. E. Davis. (1997). "Supervisee Empowerment: Does Gender Make a Difference?" *Counselor Education and Supervision,* 36:305–17.

Granello, D.H. and R. J. Hazler. (1998). "A Developmental Rationale for Curriculum Order and Teaching Styles in Counselor Education." *Counsellor Education and Supervision,* 38:89–105.

Green, D.R. (1998) "Investigating the Core Skills of Clinical Supervision: A Qualitative Analysis." *D. Clin.Psych.* diss., University of Leeds.

Harris, T., L. B. Moret, J. Gale and K. L. Kampmeyer. (2001). "Therapists' Gender Assumptions and How these Assumptions Influence Therapy." *Journal of Feminist Family Therapy,* 12(2/3):33–59.

Hawkins, P. and R.Shohet. (2000). *Supervision in the Helping Professions.* 2nd ed. Buckingham: Open University Press.

Haynes, R., G. Corey and P. Moulton. (2003). *Clinical Supervision in the Helping Professions: A Practical Guide.* Forest Grove, CA: Thomson Brooks/Cole.

Henwood, K. and A. Phoenix. (1999). "'Race' in Psychology, Teaching the Subject," in *Ethnic and Racial Studies Today.* Edited by M. Bulmer and J. Solomos. London: Routledge.

Hess, A.K., ed. (1980). *Psychotherapy Supervision: Theory, Research and Practice.* New York: Wiley.

Hess, A.K. (1987). "Psychotherapy Supervision: Stages, Buber, and a Theory of Relationship." *Professional Psychology: Research and Practice,* 18:251–59.

Holloway, E.L. and B. E. Wampold. (1983). "Patterns of Verbal Behavior and Judgments of Satisfaction in the Supervision Interview." *Journal of Counseling Psychology,* 28:373–76.

Holloway, E.L. (1995). *Clinical Supervision: A Systems Approach.* London: Sage.

Holloway, E.L. (1997). "Structures for the Analysis and Teaching of Supervision," in *Handbook of Psychotherapy Supervision.* Edited by C.E. Watkins. Chichester: Wiley.

Holloway, E.L. (1999). "A Framework for Supervision Training" in E.L. Holloway and M. Carroll, *Training Counselling Supervisors.* London: Sage.

Holloway, E.L. and M. Carroll. (1999). *Training Counselling Supervisors.* London: Sage.

Jacobs, M. (1996). *In Search of Supervision.* Buckingham: Open University Press.

Judy, D.W. (2004). "Wisdom from the Desert: Qualifications for Supervisors of Spiritual Directors." *Journal of Supervision and Training in Ministry,* 24:70–82.

Kadushin, A. (1985). *Supervision in Social Work.* 2nd ed. New York: Columbia University Press.

Kadushin, A. (1992). *Supervision in Social Work.* 2nd ed. New York: Columbia University Press.

Knapp, S. and L.Vandecreek. (1997). "Ethical and Legal Aspects of Clinical Supervision." Pages 589–602 in *Handbook of Psychotherapy Supervision.* Edited by C. Watkins. New York: Wiley.

Kolb, D.A. (1984). *Experiential Learning: Experience as a Source of Learning and Development.* 2nd ed. Englewood Cliffs, NJ: Prentice-Hall.

Krathwohl, D. R., B. S. Bloom and B. Masia. (1964). *Taxonomy of Educational Objectives, Handbook 2: The Affective Domain.* New York: Longman.

Ladany, N., M. G. Constantine and E. W. Hofheinz. (1997). "Supervisee Multicultural Case Conceptualisation Ability and Self-Reported Multicultural Competence as Functions of Supervisee Racial Identity and Supervisor Focus." *Journal of Counseling Psychology,* 44:284–93.

Lawton, B. and C. Feltham, eds. (2000). *Taking Supervision Forward.* London: Sage.

Leddick, G. R. and J. M. Bernard. (1980) "The History of Supervision: A Critical Review." *Counselor Education and Supervision,* 19(3):186–96.

Loganbill, C., E. Hardy, and U. Delworth. (1982). "Supervision: A Conceptual Model." *The Counseling Psychologist,* 10:3–42.

Lopez, S. (1997). "Cultural Competence in Psychotherapy: A Guide for Clinicians and their Supervisors." Pages 570–88 in *Handbook of Psychotherapy Supervision.* Edited by C.E. Watkins. New York: Wiley.

Martindale, B., et al, eds. (1997). *Supervision and Its Vicissitudes.* London: Karnac.

Martinez, R.P. and E. L. Holloway. (1997). "The Supervision Relationship in Multicultural Training," in *Multicultural Counseling Competencies: Assessment, Education, Training and Supervision.* Edited by D.B. Pope-Davis and H.L.K. Coleman. London: Sage.

McNeill, B.W. and V. Worthen. (1989). "The Parallel Process in Psychotherapy Supervision." *Professional Psychology: Research and Practice,* 20:329–33.

Mezirow, J. & Associates (2000). *Learning as Transformation: Critical Perspectives on a Theory in Progress.* San Francisco: Jossey-Bass.

Milne, D. and V. Oliver. (2000). "Flexible Formats of Supervision: Description, Evaluation and Implementation."*Journal of Mental Health,* 9(3):291–304.

Milne, D.L. and I. James. (2002). "The Observed Impact of Training on Competence in Clinical Supervision." *British Journal of Clinical Psychology,* 41:55–72.

Morrison,T. (1993). *Staff Supervision in Social Care: An Action Learning Approach.* Harlow: Longman.

Munro, P. (1995). "Speculations: Negotiating a Feminist Supervision Identity." Pages 97–114 in *Repositioning Feminism and Education: Perspectives on Education for Social Change.* Edited by Westport, CT: Bergin and Garvey.

Munson, C.E. (2002). *Handbook of Clinical Social Work Supervision.* 3rd ed. New York, London, Oxford: The Haworth Press.

Nicholls, G. (2002). *Developing Teaching and Learning in Higher Education.* London and New York: Routledge-Falmer.

Norcross, J. C. and R. P. Halgin. (1997). "Integrative Approaches to Psychotherapy Supervision." Pages 203–22 in *Handbook of Psychotherapy Supervision.* Edited by J. C. E.Watkins. New York: Wiley.

Ooijen, E. van. (2003). *Clinical Supervision Made Easy.* Edinburgh: Churchill Livingstone.

Page, S. and V. Wosket. (2001). *Supervising the Counsellor: A Cyclical Model.* 2nd ed. Hove: Brunner-Routledge.

Peace, S.D. and N.A. Sprinthall. (1998). "Training School Counselors to Supervise Beginning Counselors: Theory, Research and Practice." *Professional School Counseling,* 1(5):2–8.

Perfect, T.J. and B. L. Schwartz. (2002). *Applied Metacognition.* Cambridge: Cambridge University Press.

Pickvance, D. (1997). "Becoming a Supervisor," in *Supervision of Psychotherapy and Counselling*. Edited by G. Shipton. Buckingham: Open University Press.

Pintrich, P.R. and G. M. Sinatra, eds. (2003). *Intentional Conceptual Change*. Mahwah, NJ: Lawrence Erlbaum Associates.

Pope-Davis, D.B. and H. L. K. Coleman, eds. (1997). *Multicultural Counseling Competencies: Assessment, Education, Training and Supervision*. London: Sage.

Powell, D.J. and A. Brodsky. (2004). *Supervision in Alcohol and Drug Abuse Counseling: Principles, Models, Methods*. Rev. ed. San Francisco: Jossey-Bass.

Prieto, L.R. (1996). "Group Supervision: Still Widely Practiced but Poorly Understood." *Counselor Education and Supervision*, 35(4):295–307.

Pritchard, J. (2000). *Good Practice in Supervision: Statutory and Voluntary Organisations*. London & Philadelphia: Jessica Kingsley Publishers.

Proctor, B. (2000). *Group Supervision: A Guide to Creative Practice*.London: Sage.

Proctor, B., (1986). "Supervision: A Co-Operative Exercise in Accountability," in *Enabling and Ensuring*.Edited by M. Maren and M. Payne. Leicester: National Youth Bureau and Council for Education and Training in Youth and Community Work.

Prouty, A. (2001). "Experiencing Feminist Family Therapy Supervision." *Journal of Feminist Family Therapy*, 12(4):171–203.

Ricoeur, P. (1967). *The Symbolism of Evil*. Boston: Beacon Press.

Ronnestad, M.H., D. E. Orlinsky, B.K. Parks and J. D. Davis. (1997). "Supervisors of Psychotherapy: Mapping Experience Level and Supervisory Confidence." *European Psychologist*, 2(3):191–201.

Russell, R.K. and T. Petrie. (1994). "Issues in Training Effective Supervisors." *Applied and Preventive Psychology*, 3:27–42.

Scaife, J. (2001). *Supervision in the Mental Health Professions: A Practitioner's Guide*. Hove: Brunner-Routledge.

Schön, D.A. (1983). *The Reflective Practitioner: How Professionals Think in Action*. New York: Basic Books.

Schön, D.A. (1986). *Educating the Reflective Practitioner*. San Francisco: Jossey-Bass.

Schön, D.A. (1991). *The Reflective Practitioner: How Professional Think in Action*. Aldershot: Avebury.

Schulte, H.M., M. J. Hall, D. Bienenfeld, et al., eds. (1997). "Liability and Accountability in Psychotherapy Supervision: A Review, Survey, and Proposal." *Academic Psychiatry*, 21(3):133–40.

Shipton, G., ed. (1997). *Supervision of Psychotherapists and Counsellors: Making a Place for Thinking.*. Buckingham: Open University Press.

Sims, R.R. and S. J. Sims, eds. (1995). *The Importance of Learning Styles: Understanding the Implications for Learning, Course Design, and Education*. Westport, CT: Greenwood Press.

Sloan, G. (1999). "Good Characteristics of a Clinical Supervisor: A Community Mental Health Nurse Perspective." *Journal of Advanced Nursing*, 30(3):713–22.

Steere, D.A., ed. (1989). *The Supervision of Pastoral Care*. Louisville: Westminster John Knox Press.

Stoltenberg, C.D., B. McNeill and U. Delworth. (1998). *IDM Supervision: An Integrated Developmental Model for Supervising Counselors and Therapists*. San Francisco: Jossey-Bass.

Sweeney, G., P. Webley and A. Treacher. (2001). "Supervision in Occupational Therapy. Part 1: The Supervisor's Anxieties." *British Journal of Occupational Therapy Special Issue*, 64(7):337–45.

Szecsödy, I. (1990). *The Learning Process in Psychotherapy Supervision*. Academic Dissertation Monograph. Stockholm: Karolinska Institute.

Szecsödy, I. (1994). "Supervision: A Complex Tool for Training." *Scandinavian Psychoanalytic Review*, 17:119–29.

Szecsödy, I (1997). "(How) Is Learning Possible in Supervision?" in *Supervision and its Vicissitudes*. Edited by B. Martindale, et al. London: Karnac, 101–16.

Tudor, K. (2002), "Transactional Analysis Supervision or Supervision Analyzed Transactionally?" *Transactional Analysis Journal*, 32(1):39–55.

Wallerstein, R.S., ed. (1981). *Becoming a Psychoanalyst. A Study of Psychoanalytic Supervision*. New York: International Universities Press.

Wallerstein, R.S. (1997). Forward to *Supervision and its Vicissitudes*, by B. Martindale, et al., eds. London: Karnac.

Watkins, C.E. Jr., ed. (1997). *Handbook of Psychotherapy Supervision*. New York: Wiley.

Weimer, M. (2002). *Learner-Centred Teaching: Five Key Changes to Practice*. San Francisco: Jossey-Bass.

Weingart, P. and N. Stehr. (2000). *Practising Interdisciplinarity*. Toronto, Buffalo, London: Toronto University Press.

Wheeler, S. and D. King. (2001). *Supervising Counsellors: Issues of Responsibility*. London: Sage.

White, E., et al, eds. (1998). "Clinical Supervision: Insider Reports of a Private World." *Journal of Advanced Nursing*, 28(1):185–92.

Yegdich, T. (1999). "Lost in the Crucible of Supportive Clinical Supervision: Supervision Is Not Therapy." *Journal of Advanced Nursing*, 29(5):1265–75.

Yorks, L. and E. Kasl. (2002). *Collaborative Inquiry as a Strategy for Adult Learning*. San Francisco: Jossey-Bass.

Yun Dai, D. and R. J. Sternberg, eds. (2004). *Motivation, Emotion, and Cognition: Integrative Perspectives on Intellectual Functioning and Development*. Mahwah, NJ: Lawrence Erlbaum Associates.

Yuval Davis, N. (1994). "Women, Ethnicity and Empowerment." Feminism and Psychology, 4(1):179–98.

Zalcman, M.J. and W. F. Cornell. (1983). "A Bilateral Model for Clinical Supervision." *Transactional Analysis Journal*, 13:112–23.

A Select Bibliography from ERIC Digest

❯ (1988). *Critical Thinking Skills and Teacher Education*. ED297003 ERIC Digest 3-88. ERIC Clearinghouse on Teacher Education Washington DC. http://www.ericdigests.org/pre-929/critical.htm (accessed 25/03/2010).

❯ Benshoff, J.M. (1994). *Peer Consultation as a Form of Supervision*. ED372352 ERIC Digest. ERIC Clearinghouse on Counseling and Student Services Greensboro NC. http://www.ericdigests.org/1995-1/peer.htm (accessed 25/03/2010).

❯ Bernard, J. M. (1994). *Ethical and Legal Dimensions of Supervision.* ED372349 ERIC Digest. ERIC Clearinghouse on Counseling and Student Services Greensboro NC. http://www.ericdigests.org/1995-1/legal.htm (accessed 25/03/2010).

❯ Blakey, E. and S. Spence. (1990). *Developing Metacognition.* ED327218 ERIC Digest. ERIC Clearinghouse on Information Resources Syracuse NY. http://www.ericdigests.org/pre-9218/developing.htm (accessed 25/03/2010).

❯ Borders, L. DiAnne (1994). *The Good Supervisor.* ED372350 ERIC Digest. ERIC Clearinghouse on Counseling and Student Services Greensboro NC. http://www.ericdigests.org/1995-1/good.htm (accessed 25/03/2010).

❯ Bradley, L. J. and L. J. Gould. (1994). *Supervisee Resistance.* ED372344 ERIC Digest. ERIC Clearinghouse on Counseling and Student Services Greensboro NC. http://www.ericdigests.org/1995-1/resistance.htm (accessed 25/03/2010).

❯ Carroll, M. F. (1994). *Counselling Supervision: International Perspectives.* ED372358 ERIC Digest. ERIC Clearinghouse on Counseling and Student Services Greensboro NC. http://www.ericdigests.org/1995-1/international.htm (accessed 25/03/2010).

❯ Cashwell, C. S. (1994). *Interpersonal Process Recall.* ED372342 ERIC Digest. ERIC Clearinghouse on Counseling and Student Services Greensboro NC. http://www.ericdigests.org/1995-1/recall.htm (accessed 25/03/2010).

❯ Claxton, C. S. and P. H. Murrell. (1988). *Learning Styles.* ED301143 ERIC Digest. ERIC Clearinghouse on Higher Education Washington DC. http://www.ericdigests.org/pre-9210/learning.htm (accessed 25/03/2010).

❯ Cryder, A. Petro et al eds. (1994). *Supervision of Marriage and Family Counselors.* ED372354 ERIC Digest. ERIC Clearinghouse on Counseling and Student Services Greensboro NC. http://www.ericdigests.org/1995-1/family.htm (accessed 25/03/2010).

❯ Dye, A. (1994). *The Supervisory Relationship.* ED372343 ERIC Digest. ERIC Clearinghouse on Counseling and Student Services Greensboro NC. http://www.ericdigests.org/1995-1/relationship.htm (accessed 25/03/2010).

❯ Fong, M. L. (1994). *Multicultural Issues in Supervision.* ED372346 ERIC Digest. ERIC Clearinghouse on Counseling and Student Services Greensboro NC. http://www.ericdigests.org/1995-1/supervision.htm (accessed 25/03/2010).

❯ Harris, M. B. Colvin (1994). *Supervisory Evaluation and Feedback.* ED372348 ERIC Digest. ERIC Clearinghouse on Counseling and Student Services Greensboro NC. http://www.ericdigests.org/1995-1/feedback.htm (accessed 25/03/2010).

❯ Hart, G. M. (1994). *Strategies and Methods of Effective Supervision.* ED372341 ERIC Digest. ERIC Clearinghouse on Counseling and Student Services Greensboro NC. http://www.ericdigests.org/1995-1/methods.htm (accessed 25/03/2010).

❯ Henderson, P. (1994). *Administrative Skills in Counseling Supervision.* ED372356 ERIC Digest. ERIC Clearinghouse on Counseling and Student Services Greensboro, NC. http://www.ericdigests.org/1995-1/skills.htm (accessed 25/03/2010).

❯ Juhnke, G. A. and J. R. Culbreth, (1994). *Clinical Supervision in Addictions Counseling: Special Challenges and Solutions.* ED372355 ERIC Digest. ERIC Clearinghouse on Counseling and Student Services Greensboro NC. http://www.ericdigests.org/1995-1/clinical.htm (accessed 25/03/2010).

> Leddick, G. R. (1994). *Models of Clinical Supervision.* ED372340 ERIC Digest. ERIC Clearinghouse on Counseling and Student Services Greensboro NC. http://www.ericdigests.org/1995-1/models.htm (accessed 25/03/2010).

> Locke, D. C. (1993). *Multicultural Counseling.* ED357316 ERIC Digest. ERIC Clearinghouse on Counseling and Personnel Services Ann Arbor MI. http://www.ericdigests.org/1993/counseling.htm (accessed 25/03/2010).

> Paisley, P. O. (1994). *Gender Issues in Supervision.* ED372345 ERIC Digest. ERIC Clearinghouse on Counseling and Student Services Greensboro NC. http://www.ericdigests.org/1995-1/issues.htm (accessed 25/03/2010).

> Potts, B. (1994). *Strategies for Teaching Critical Thinking.* ED385606 ERIC/AE Digest. ERIC Clearinghouse on Assessment and Evaluation Washington DC. http://www.ericdigests.org/1996-1/critical.htm (accessed 25/03/2010).

> Sumerel, M. B. (1994). *Parallel Process in Supervision.* ED372347 ERIC Digest. ERIC Clearinghouse on Counseling and Student Services Greensboro NC. http://www.ericdigests.org/1995-1/process.htm (accessed 25/03/2010).

> Werstlein, P. O. (1994). *Fostering Counselors' Development in Group Supervision.* ED372351 ERIC Digest. ERIC Clearinghouse on Counseling and Student Services Greensboro NC. http://www.ericdigests.org/1995-1/group.htm (accessed 25/03/2010).

CHAPTER

9

∾

An Integrated Model of Supervision in Training Spiritual Directors

ﬁ *Janet K. Ruffing* ﬂ

This chapter is a further development of an article which first appeared in *Presence*, "An Integrated Model of Supervision in Training Spiritual Directors" (Vol. 9, No. 1, 2003). Used with permission.

Introduction

The development of models and skills for training spiritual directors has gradually evolved over the past twenty-five years. The Center for Religious Development led the way in their original program by accepting spiritual- direction interns who had already completed a unit of Clinical Pastoral Education and who had been engaged in offering spiritual direction for some time. This approach relied on tools and skills initially developed for training pastoral counselors or chaplains. They employed the methods of process or case notes, taped interviews, verbatims, as well as individual and group supervision. All of these methods focused on the experience of directors giving spiritual direction.

Initially, a sharp distinction was made between consultation and supervision. Consultation referred to specialized information about the directee that a director might seek from an expert. This might be specific information about and approaches to a particular psychological situation such as issues faced by an adult child of an alcoholic or to spiritual matters such as the use of contemplative prayer by a directee. Supervision, for its part, referred to issues and behaviors evoked in the spiritual director by particular directees. These included such things as recognizing and addressing countertransference toward the directee, which inhibited the director's normally skilled responses to the directee, or psychological or spiritual issues of the director. The Center for Religious Development model of spiritual direction also emphasized that the focus of spiritual direction is the religious experience of the directee and that one of the most important skills of a spiritual director is a contemplative attitude toward the religious experience of the directee (Barry and Connolly 1982). Maureen Conroy, a graduate of this program, further developed the CRD model through her book, *Looking into the Well: Supervision of Spiritual Directors* (1995). In that book, she wrote descriptions of the supervision process, offered helpful models of verbatims, and identified five key areas of the director's experience that potentially can become the content of supervision sessions. Conroy's model of supervision for spiritual direction emphasizes a contemplative approach to the process of spiritual direction and the supervisory process. She focuses on (1) the interior movements within the director; (2) the development of the director's contemplative attitude and approach; (3) the way a director's personal issues are stirred during sessions (countertransference); (4) moral, theological, or cultural differences between director and directee, and; (5) the ongoing relationship between director and directee.

In addition to the two models for supervision developed by The Center for Religious Development and Maureen Conroy, I propose a third model which integrates the strengths of the models just described with several more variables in the supervisory relationship. During my eighteen years of supervising spiritual directors at Fordham University and elsewhere, I have never been able to confine my explorations with intern directors to their experience as directors alone, especially in the early stages of their experience as directors. In other words, I supervise differently depending on the level of skill and experience a director initially brings to the practicum. At the beginning of the practicum, I am constantly monitoring the directors' understanding of their directees and their application of the standard helping skills—described in Gerard Egan's *Skilled Helper* (1986) or Clara Hill and Karen O'Brien's *Helping Skills* (1999) for example—that were learned and practiced during pre-practicum courses. Finally, a psychologist is an integral part of the supervisory team that I propose. Supervisors are tracking the psychological issues intern directors are encountering in their directees, their transference-countertransference experiences with them, and the supervisors' own transference-countertransference experiences with super-visees. Supervisors also attend to the directors' contemplative attitude and presence, as well as the content areas Conroy so helpfully describes. In this expanded model, supervisors work for integration of the psycho-spiritual dynamics of both the intern directors and their directees.

The most helpful overall framework for individual supervision of spiritual directors upon which this third model is derived is Barry Estadt's description of supervision in the pastoral counseling context (Estadt 1987). He describes the stages in the supervisory relationship as itself a parallel process for the director. The supervisory relationship has the same stages of development as the spiritual-direction relationship (establishing the working relationship, the work of the established alliance, and concluding the supervisory alliance) and often models for the director the same skills and helping processes of exploration, insight, and action possibilities that are employed when facilitating spiritual direction. In comparison to earlier models, Estadt's schema better identifies concerns supervisors typically encounter when working with beginning directors. Estadt's complete chart (adapted to supervising inexperienced spiritual directors) appears below.

THE STAGES OF SUPERVISION			
STAGES	Stage 1 Early Phase Building the Alliance	Stage 2 Middle Phase The Working Alliance	Stage 3 Final Phase Concluding the Alliance
SUPERVISOR FACILITATES BY	Acceptance Empathy (Primary) Genuineness	Empathy (Advanced) Immediacy of Interaction Supervisor-Director Supervisor- Directee Director-Directee Parallel Process	Collegial Affirmation and Evaluation
SUPERVISORY TASKS	Learning Contract Trust Relationship	Director Issues Skill Acquisition Self-knowledge Direction Capacity Ethical Sensitivity Pastoral Identity Director-Directee Issues Knowledge of the Directee Direction Relationship Supervisor-Director Issues Supervisability Supervisory Competence	Summation Termination

Generalized Dynamic of Supervision

Most supervisors agree that the focus of spiritual-direction supervision is the experience of the director during spiritual-direction sessions. The purpose of supervision is to help directors explore their new experience—attending leading to awareness. This evocative, contemplative exploration focuses on the director's interior experiencing. In addition, the feelings evoked from the director role-playing the directee frequently yield insight into the directee's experience. Finally, the insight or new perspective gained during these sessions leads to personalizing and integration. The director's new insight provides the basis for potential new responses to similar situations. Personalizing includes the director's arriving at new responses out of his/her own unique personality as well as embracing behavior change in the direction process, such as refraining from advice-giving, teaching, or inappropriate self-disclosure. These inappropriate behaviors may then be replaced by ones that facilitate their directees' dynamic self-exploration, leading to their own insights and eventually personalizing or behavior change. This cycle is repeated over and over in supervision, modeling for the director the same skills needed in direction sessions.

Director's Issues

Estadt's categories under Director Issues clarify several supervisory tasks for spiritual- direction supervision that are not identified as sharply in the other frameworks. At the beginning of the practicum, supervisors interview the potential directees' interns they will be seeing during the practicum. Potential directees are referred to other growth opportunities if the supervisor is unable to discover a positive and realistic motivation for spiritual direction and a sufficiently developed personal relationship with God. Although mistakes are inevitable, supervisors have an ethical responsibility to insure that intern directors do no harm to their directees. Supervisors initially need to pay a great deal of attention to the way directors are interpreting the unfolding content of their directees' disclosures. Are the directors reasonably accurate and focused on spiritual-direction content, while also being aware of their directees' entire life context in a holistic way? Are they patient enough to discover their directees' internal and external resources or do they assume they don't have many? Do the directors have the necessary knowledge to respond to their directees' issues? Is this knowledge about prayer or normal dynamics of growth in the spiritual life? Is this knowledge psychological—recognizing serious depression or suicidal thoughts, for instance? Do they have sufficient facility with Scripture to be able to support their directees' scripturally based prayer?

Initial Stages of Supervision

The first supervision session usually focuses on the experience the intern directors are having in their initial interviews with their directees, reassuring them in order to reduce anxiety in the new role, and discovering whether or not directors have been able to elicit and respond to some aspect of their directees' religious experience. Supervisors encourage the director to make their initial connection with their directees through contemplative presence and response to some present-moment aspect of the directees' spiritual experience. Even in this initial stage, when anxiety is normally high and surprise is often the order of the day, some directors report being deeply moved by and drawn into the directees' experience of God. They are beginning to feel their innate responses to the sacred mystery their directees experience and are calmed and consoled by that. In addition, as supervisors, they look for some resemblance between the directors' assessment of their directees and their own sense of the same directees. Supervision entails working with the directors' perceptions of and initial understandings of their directees. Supervisors look for the interns' developing knowledge of their directees' characteristic religious experience and personality styles. They assess how well they are able to appropriately draw on the helping skills they learned prior to the practicum. Some interns have unique ways of responding to their directees. One new director spontaneously expressed his felt response to his directee's spiritual narrative with lovely metaphors which exactly captured the felt tone and content of the directee's statements without actually naming the feeling. It was as if metaphor spoke directly to metaphor. Supervisors notice and affirm such creativity and delicacy, helping directors recognize and appreciate these natural gifts.

Directors in the Fordham program which I directed have had forty-two hours of a helping-skills class which typically covers the skills of reflective listening, exploration of feelings, concreteness, genuineness, basic and advanced empathy, and sometimes focusing. Directors usually work so hard at learning to reflect feelings and content to their directees that they have only just begun to connect information from session to session and to offer tentative, beginning interpretations leading to insight. They have usually not yet learned how to invite the directee to move from insight to behavior change or another form of personalizing the insight. Thus, at the beginning of the practicum, intern directors need to consolidate their helping skills and apply them in the service of spiritual direction, choosing to explore the feelings which lead to discovering their directees' religious experience or exploring the feelings and reactions of the directees in response to their consoling experiences. Supervisors probe for the reasons directors chose to focus on some content areas but not others. Are they problem-centered or God-centered? Are they able to inhabit the contemplative attitude as described by Barry and Connolly (1982) or Tilden Edwards (1995)? Do they have a feel for where to look for God in their directees' experience and how to support their directees' responses? Can they use their skills of attending and exploring in this sensitive area? Are they beginning to embody a contemplative approach to spiritual direction?

Most of the interns in the Fordham program already have a pastoral or professional identity other than that of spiritual director. They grow in self-knowledge as they begin to recognize that they are more comfortable with another role which has attuned them to want to teach, give advice, mother, reconcile, or catechize. Throughout the supervisory process, the director's self-knowledge deepens and grows. Directors are referred back to their own spiritual direction to explore and resolve any spiritual issues that are uncovered in supervision and which may have been triggered in their new role as director. Some become envious of their directees' flourishing prayer life and are invited to deepen their own. Others move away from their directees' consoling experiences because they are currently experiencing God's absence instead of closeness. Intern directors are referred to counseling or therapeutic relationships if their own existential issues are impairing or complicating their work. Some directors tend to emphasize as their principal skill the exploration of feelings in their work with directees. Others, who are more cognitive in orientation, tend to emphasize skills that lead to insight. As directors grow to understand their tendency toward a special interest, they can more consciously integrate a balance between the two skills and phases of the helping process. Those who rush to insight, offering it ready-made for their directees, can learn to slow down and spend enough time in the exploration phase so that directees can arrive at insight about themselves through facilitation rather than through announcement. Those who are more adept at lifting up the feelings can learn from the insight-specialists that feelings lead to shifts in relationships and changes of behavior. Every feeling does not necessarily need to be explored. These directors can begin to move toward interpretation and awareness leading to insight. Once both phases are integrated, directors are free to shift their focus to explore possible behavior changes and offer the appropriate support directees need to implement and consolidate those changes in their lives.

The director's ability to function helpfully unfolds throughout the entire practicum. For some, ability is apparent from the beginning; for others, it will take the whole practicum to grasp what the process is about and how to participate in it. In both pre-practicum courses and in the practicum, supervisors encourage directors to recognize not only moral issues as they emerge in their own or their directees' experience but also to recognize societal or systemic forms of injustice which contribute to the suffering of their directees. We hope directors discover how to accompany their directees through exploration and insight so that directees are empowered to make their own moral judgments and respond to possibilities of addressing situations of injustice.

Finally, by the end of the practicum, supervisors test to see whether a director has a new identity as a spiritual director distinct from other pastoral or professional ones. Are they still attracted to this ministry? Has this been affirmed through the experience with their directees and in supervision? Supervisors also do careful work with boundaries and with professional pastoral ethics related to this new role as a spiritual director for the intern. Throughout the practicum, this new identity is slowly or rapidly unfolding and is received with ambivalence, tentativeness, and often welcome.

Director-Directee Issues

In Estadt's framework, the category of director-directee issues has only two subdivisions: knowledge of the client, and the direction relationship itself. The first subdivision, knowledge of the client, easily encompasses Maureen Conroy's attention to interior movements in both the directee and director and the whole process of discernment vis-a-vis the directees' experience. To these dynamics, Fordham supervisors add a holistic assessment which takes into account physical, situational, psychological, and systemic realities which affect the spirituality and religious experience of the directee. Thus, directors keep the contexts of their directees in awareness, yielding a more realistic interpretation of their directees' spiritual dimension.

The second subdivision, the direction relationship, includes Conroy's cautions about how directors' issues affect their responses to directees—including a director's personal issues and their experience of interior movements; moral, theological, or cultural differences between the director and the directee; the development of a contemplative attitude; and the overall quality of the relationship with the directee.

Supervisor-Director Issues

Estadt's third set of supervisory tasks revolve around supervisor-director issues. After many practicums, supervisors learn to screen potential directors for their capacity to participate in and benefit from the supervision experience as well as for their capacity to accompany directees. Pre-practicum case work is aimed at helping the potential director to notice and become aware of spontaneous reactions to directees' personal narratives and to identify key aspects of the new director's spiritual journey and present growing edges. Twenty potential directors will have twenty different responses and interpretations of the case material that serves in provoking their reflections and reactions. In both the practicum and the pastoral counseling and spiritual-direction skills course, supervisors look for the director's openness to influence from peers and teachers. Are they able to go deeper in noticing their own reactions and wondering about their sources? Are they aware of their own inner process and can they begin to articulate it? Can they receive both negative and positive feedback? In both the pre-practicum courses and the practicum, usually the most spiritually and pastorally experienced interns (the most naturally gifted directors) are the most open to reflecting on their experience and the most amenable to influence in the supervisory process. The least naturally gifted and the most psychologically distressed are frequently the least able to receive a clear recommendation that their gifts lie elsewhere and that they should not continue to offer spiritual direction to others.

Those directors who most readily accept supervision develop supervisory competence. They learn from everything—successes and mistakes. They know when they need help and ask for it. They reflect deeply on their experience with directees and become increasingly able to internalize the supervisory process. Just making notes in preparation for supervision often reveals a great deal of initial insight for them and they recognize where and how they might have made better responses. They recognize when the complexity of a given situation requires consultation and more specific knowledge. They are usually the most able to explore their own reactions deeply enough to recognize, with help, their countertransferential reactions and learn from them.

The Middle Phase of Supervision

Estadt emphasizes that advanced empathy and immediacy are the principal skills used by the supervisor in the middle phase of the supervisory process. The supervisor's ability to receive directors just as they are, gifted or struggling, easy or difficult to be with, is expressed through advanced empathic responses to the directors' feelings about their experience. Since supervisors never know what is going to come up in a session, the process—just as in spiritual direction itself—is often intuitive and immediate. Supervisors can help directors who are unable to name complex feelings stirred up by their directees through sharing what the supervisor might feel with this particular directee. The supervisor may role-play with the director to get a more fully embodied sense of what might be going on. The supervisor's spontaneity, flexibility, and perhaps broader repertoire of responses to the director often models the way it feels when directors are free both to be entirely themselves and also to serve their directees' growth. Each supervisor will have her or his own unique style and emphasis, as will directors.

Ending Phase of Supervision

Concluding the supervisory relationship provides wonderful opportunities to understand consciously the feelings associated with the termination phase of both the spiritual-direction relationship and the supervisory relationship. The supervisory process allows space and time to reflect on endings and how to summarize, affirm, and potentially ease intern directors into both processes. If the parallel processes between supervision and spiritual direction are not experientially clear earlier in the process, they surely are by the end.

Conclusion

In an effort to expand the way supervisors understand their work with spiritual directors, especially in the practicum phase of a spiritual-direction program, I have proposed an integrated model of supervision. The model integrates the original insights of The Center for Spiritual Development, Maureen Conroy's insights, and Barry Estadt's unifying framework of supervision with pastoral counselors, which includes the structured approach to helping skills development that is part of some pastoral counseling programs. The model I have proposed enables supervisors to integrate more easily within the supervisory process by focusing on both the spiritual dimensions and contemplative approaches required for spiritual direction, with significant attention to helping skills and psychological dynamics. It advances a theoretical model of supervision that recognizes different stages in the supervisory process itself and that takes into account the differences between inexperienced and more experienced spiritual directors.

Bibliography

Barry, William and William Connolly. 1982. *The Practice of Spiritual Direction*, chapter 4. New York: Seabury.

Cleary, Miriam. "Societal Context for Supervision." Presence 4 (October 1997):12ff. The "Experience Cycle" is used during the pre-practicum course.

Conroy, Maureen. 1995. *Looking Into the Well: Supervision of Spiritual Directors*. Chicago: Loyola University Press.

Edwards, Tilden. 1995. "Immediate Givenness to God in the Spiritual Direction Relationship." Presence 1 (May 1995): 5–12.

Egan, Gerard. 1986. *The Skilled Helper: A Systemic Approach to Effective Helping.* Monterey: Brooks/Cole.

Estadt, Barry. 1987. "The Core Process of Supervision" In *The Art of Clinical Supervision: A Pastoral Counseling Perspective.* New York: Paulist Press.

Fitchett, George. 1993. *Assessing Spiritual Needs: A Guide for Caregivers.* Minneapolis: Fortress Press. I have developed a spiritual assessment section in greater detail for spiritual directors. This tool is used in the pre-practicum course.

Hill, Clara E. and Karen M. O'Brien. 1999. *Helping Skills: Facilitating Exploration, Insight, and Action.* Washington, DC: American Psychological Association.

Chapter

10

∽

A Process Framework for
Learning in a New Era of Supervision

∽ *Robert M. Moore* ∾

O
n coming into her new post as a residential social worker in a home for adolescents, Jessica was told that the young person who was to be her first client had filed complaints against every staff member who had previously worked with him and that she needed to be very careful. Armed with this "knowledge" she described in supervision how she found herself wary of him, holding back, desperately trying to be what she described as "particularly nice to him."

Introduction

Constructed on a philosophy of learning, supervision is emerging as a distinct profession. If that statement is accurate, then what is so distinctive about what supervisors do? In this chapter, I will explore the context within which supervisory practice is evolving and suggest a "process framework" that describes the activities of supervisors as they facilitate learning for supervisees. Within a culture of learning, supervisees are encouraged to view their work through the lens of an extended epistemology (Reason and Bradbury 2001) that values emotional, theoretical, and practical knowing. They are invited to engage with the intense empathic impact their clients have on them, draw meaning from that experience, and apply it in their practice. The non-shaming learning environment of the process framework is at the service of facilitating, firstly, *self-awareness* through reflexivity; secondly, *other-awareness* through empathy; and finally, *therapeutic awareness* through reiterative empathy. I will use the experience of supervision with Jessica as an example of facilitating learning and as a way to carry the reader through the steps of the process framework.

The Dawning of a New Era

Carroll (1996) has suggested that the emergence of supervision as a profession followed three major developmental stages. Born initially within psychoanalysis, supervision quickly adapted, in its second stage, to the perspectives of the various counseling models that flourished with the fragmentation of the therapeutic world. The third stage involved the incorporation of developmental models of how supervisor and supervisee learn, including the various social roles assumed in the supervisory relationship. Throughout the development of the profession, many authors formulated models of supervision that reflected distinctive perspectives on the fledgling profession. These include, among others, a "cyclical" model (Page and Wosket 1994), a "systemic" model (Holloway 1995), a "generic tasks" model (Carroll 1996), a "process" model (Hawkins and Shohet 2000), and an "integrative relational" model (Gilbert and Evans 2000). The development of these models has allowed supervision to increasingly describe itself as an activity discrete from counseling and therapy while at the same time contributing to the quality of therapeutic practitioners' work (Alonso 1985). Supervision has been liberated from the "theories of truth" underpinning psychotherapy and counseling (Mahrer 2004) through the establishment of a much more appropriate alliance with theories of learning.

The process framework (Moore 2005) presented here does not compete with the range of alternative models of supervision, which represent "broad perspective[s] that capture both processes and range of functions" (Page and Wosket 1994: 29). Pragmatically the framework suggests a possible "how" in response to the "what" of a model. To paraphrase Strachan:

> . . . a process framework is a step-by-step conceptual guide to what a **supervisor** does in a structured **supervision** session. It makes the process explicit, furnishes a reference point for keeping the process on track, and supports **supervisors** and **supervisees** in thinking reflexively about the learning that is unfolding or alternatively exploring the blocks to learning. (2007: 4)

A process framework, as a boundaried yet flexible container, offers a tool for reflexive learning that can be used to explore in greater depth some aspect of the supervisory process that models draw our attention to. For example it could:

1. Facilitate an in-depth exploration of the "basic affective relationship" at Stage 2 of Page and Wosket's (1994) cyclical model.
2. Outline a helpful series of steps for discerning and exploring the nature of the various relationships identified as constituting Holloway's (1995) relational system.
3. Provide a method for operationalizing each of the seven generic tasks of supervision in Carroll's (1996) linear model.
4. Act as a tool for reflection on the relational components within Hawkins and Shohet's (2000) 7-eyed model and Gilbert and Evans' (2000) integrative relational model.

As supervision stakes a claim for recognition as a profession, it is important to distinguish its philosophical basis from that of the traditional professions. Professionalism has conventionally been described as based on the concept of "technical rationality" with "four essential properties: specialised, firmly bounded, scientific and standardised" (Schön 1996: 9). Alternatively, supervision is rooted in the new professionalism of "reflection-in-action" argued for by Schön as "an epistemology of practice implicit in the artistic, intuitive processes which some practitioners do bring to situations of uncertainty, instability, uniqueness and value conflict" (1996: 19). The theory of knowledge development and learning that underpins the process framework presented in this chapter provides a methodology for this reflection-in-action. More importantly, the philosophy of supervision is also distinct from the various philosophies of human development around which the theories of therapy have been constructed. Each theory of counseling and psychotherapy is built around three concepts:

1. theoretical assumptions concerning the basic constituents of healthy human development,
2. diagnostic tools that account for the psychopathology of clients, and
3. a set of therapeutic techniques for treating the pathology (my adaptation from Greenberg and Mitchell, 1983).

Alternatively, supervision when it is built on a philosophy of learning is informed by:

1. theoretical assumptions concerning creative processes of learning,

2. an understanding of the conditions in which learning is hindered or indeed arrested altogether, and

3. a framework or set of tools for the enhancement of learning environments.

Embedded now in theories of learning, perhaps this philosophy of learning heralds the dawn of a fourth era of supervision, one characterised by "cross-professional" supervision in which skilled supervisors facilitate learning environments across a wide range of professions, an era in which supervisees bring the insights of their own professions while supervisors contribute a core set of knowledge and skills that assist supervisee learning.

The Process Framework: An Overview

Supervision might usefully be conceptualized as a participative action-research process with the action phase representing the professional practice of the supervisee and the reflective phase being that of the supervisory learning environment. While the process framework outlined in Figure 1 (Moore 2008) portrays the supervisory reflection happening between professional encounters with clients, it is hoped that over time the supervisee's capacity to reflect within each encounter will be enhanced. This mirrors Casement's (1985) development of the internal supervisor.

In Figure 1, the top line of boxes traces the client's journey between professional encounters, the bottom line traces the reflexive journey of the supervisee, while the middle line represents the professional encounters where the two paths meet. The clients bring the distressing symptoms of his emotional dilemmas (anger, pain, depression) to each encounter while the supervisees initially adopt a stance of empathic openness to the encounter. This first phase of the work is predominantly experiential, and consequently supervisees experience some of the clients' anger, pain, and depression, with a subsequent increase in their own levels of stress and anxiety.

While these feelings are overwhelming for the clients, supervision offers supervisees a reflexive space to explore the empathic impact and draw meaning out of it. Supervisees require a high degree of self-awareness to differentiate between those feelings arising from their own experiences and those given to them in empathy. Since empathic feelings always belong to both participants, rather than simply one or the other, the reflective task is one of discerning which is the predominant source. It is seldom easy to acknowledge the intense emotions that supervisees can experience empathically and so they require a safe, inquiring, and non-shaming rather than harshly critical supervisory space. Exploring the emotional impact in depth and applying their theoretical understanding helps supervisees to make sense of their own emotions and gain insight into the clients' dilemmas. This second phase is principally about understanding and learning to think feelingly (Assasgioli 1985) as experience is reflected on in the light of theory.

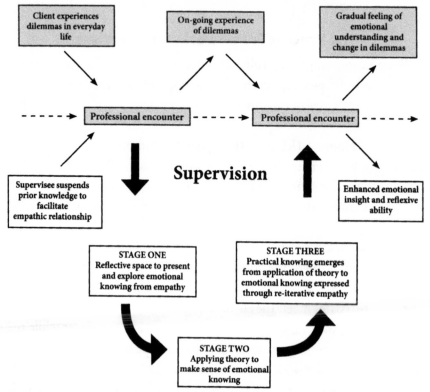

Figure 1

The meaning that emerges from professional encounters draws supervisees towards the kind of interventions that might communicate emotional understanding to their clients. At this point it is important for supervisees to remember that their clients have not gone through this reflexive process, having meanwhile returned to the on-going experience of relationships in life. While the next professional encounter is a fresh experience, it is one into which supervisees can bring a new emotional sensitivity to their clients. Engaging at a deeper emotional level provides containment and, through reiterative empathy (Stein 1916), clients gradually experience an emotional containment of their distress. This third phase of practical intervention is informed by the understanding that has emerged from reflection on the emotional experience. Supervisees, meanwhile, continue to allow the clients' emotions to impact them, attending carefully to the subtle differences in each emotional encounter. The process framework does not seek to lessen the impact of emotional connection, and supervisees of many years' practice will continue to experience intense feelings when working with distressed clients. As a participative action-research outcome, supervisees over time will have an enhanced capacity to tolerate and work creatively with the strong emotions with which their clients struggle, while clients will experience a gradual reduction of the intensity of their dilemmas.

In summary, the role of the supervisor is to facilitate learning environments within which supervisees can deepen their reflexive ways of knowing through experience, understanding, and applied knowledge. Traditional models of learning, like that of Kolb (1984), emphasize planning and enacting—followed by reflection on the action—to better inform planning for future action. This process describes what we have come to know as the "reflective practitioner." Alvesson and Skoldberg (2000) have taken this model a step further and introduced the "reflexive practitioner." Reflexivity involves attending to the complex relationship between multiple levels of knowledge production in learning. In the process framework, practitioner-generated knowledge occurs through empathic awareness and critical engagement with established theoretical perspectives, culminating in enhanced skill in the application of insights.

The reflexive development of supervisees' knowing outlined in Figure 2 below represents: a) *primary knowing* that facilitates openness to empathic impact; b) *experiential knowing* that differentiates between feelings arising from themselves and those given to them empathically by their clients; c) *presentational knowing* that allows supervisees to creatively present the client world in the supervisory space; d) *propositional knowing* that consists of the capacity to apply theoretical perspectives to the empathic experience; e) *practical knowing* that allows supervisees to apply theoretical understanding in a way that is helpful for their clients; f) a second *primary knowing* which reminds supervisees that the clients have not undertaken this reflexive journey and hence need to be open to what is brought to the next encounter; and g) a second *experiential knowing* that is sensitive to the subtle changes in the emotional experience of the client.

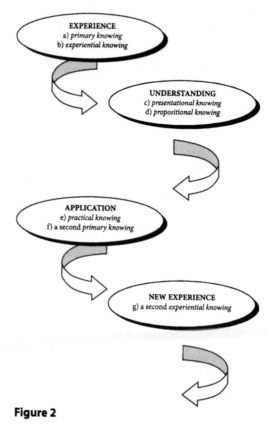

Figure 2

The Process Framework in Action

To provide an overview of the process framework in action, I will draw on my experience of supervision with Jessica, a female supervisee who—as a residential childcare social worker—presented her work with a male adolescent client who has been in care for a number of years. This narrative has necessarily been abbreviated and conflated for clarity of presentation and for the protection of identity.

The process framework for supervision, as a forum of reflexive learning, clarifies the conditions in which understanding can unfold in a culture of inquiry. It is the task of Jessica to relate her experience to her professional theory as a social worker while the supervisor maintains the non-shaming environment within which learning can emerge. Set within three phases of the process framework, the following is an example of Jessica's reflection on her experience with her client Brian.

1. Phase One: Knowing through Experience

> Jessica was told that Brian had taken out complaints against every staff member who had worked directly with him. As stated earlier, armed with this "knowledge," she found herself wary of him, holding back and trying to be what she described as "particularly nice to him." She was trying desperately not to give him any cause for complaint and recognized that her niceness was false since underneath she was afraid of him.

De Bono (1996) argues that most of our errors in judgment are caused by errors in perception because we struggle to tolerate not-knowing. Faced with the unknown we urgently seek to place it within already existing, known frameworks and to look for patterns. As soon as we think we see a familiar pattern, we stop looking for other possibilities. To counteract this tendency towards premature assumptions, De Bono argues for a "possibility system" of perception that encourages suspension of judgment, supporting the formation of various working hypotheses. Scharmer (2007) and others (Senge, Scharmer, Jaworski, and Flowers 2005) take up this dilemma of how we tolerate uncertainty sufficiently to maintain openness to the new. In contrast with previous models of learning that emphasized reflection on the past (Kolb 1984), Scharmer stresses an open, inviting, and facilitative stance towards the emerging future that:

> ❭ suspends judgment in order to see with fresh eyes,
> ❭ redirects attention in order to sense what is emerging, and
> ❭ allows one to "let-go" of what is known or desired in order to "let-come" what is emerging.

For Scharmer the key benefit of this suspension of judgment is that it enhances the capacity for "empathic listening":

> *We forget about our own agenda and begin to see how the world unfolds through someone else's eyes . . . . It is a skill that requires us to activate a different source of intelligence: the intelligence of the heart. (Scharmer 2007: 12)*

Scharmer describes this capacity as "primary knowing," a stance towards others that opens up the possibility of emotional knowing.

> *In supervision Jessica recognized that in her tendency to hold back from Brian she was viewing him from the perspective of what she had been told and struggled to be open to what new possibilities he might bring to the encounter with her. She decided to practice suspending the assumption that he would inevitably compromise her in some way and listen more closely to how she found herself feeling when she was with him.*

The suspension of assumptions inherent in primary knowing that promotes an environment of empathic listening is reflective of earlier work in therapeutic contexts. For example, in language similar to Scharmer, Greenson says of his listening that:

> *I shifted from listening and observing from the outside to listening and feeling from the inside. I permitted part of myself to become part of the patient. (1967: 421)*

This type of listening was only possible after a process of suspension, as observed by Bolognini, who sums up Greenson's views on empathy:

> *The capacity to suspend judgment, to the very limit of credulity, is what makes empathy with the patient*

possible, and will eventually lead to an understanding of the underlying movements. (2004: 47)

At this initial stage in the process framework, Jessica is invited to let go of the assumptions and attitudes that arose from her previous knowledge of Brian, which came through others rather than directly through personal experience. Failing to see beyond and beneath habitual behaviors can lead to false assumptions on the part of supervisees, blocking empathic listening and objectifying their clients rather than holding in mind the person in the here and now of the particular situation. Perhaps this is what Bion hinted at when he spoke of entering the relationship with neither "memory nor desire" (1976: 314). Primary knowing is a mindset of openness to the emerging, uniquely empathic knowing, which of its nature cannot be accurately grasped by what is already known.

> *In the next encounter with Brian, Jessica practiced holding an open mind and open heart, listening empathically through her emotions to what was being communicated by him. The conscious exchange between the two (largely the verbal narrative) provided the "text" of the encounter, while the much more subtle and important "sub-text" was made up of the emotional narrative. Attending to the sub-text allowed Jessica to be fully open to the explosion of anger and rage within her when Brian spat in her face.*

Lipps (1912–1913), the philosopher attributed with originating thinking around empathy, considered it to be a natural process ". . . after all, empathy is a varied, yet unavoidable and natural affair." Stueber (2006), basing his writing on the work of the many theorists who followed Lipps, goes a little further:

> *I will argue . . . that the renewed attention to empathy as the primary method for understanding other minds is indeed well deserved and that empathy must be regarded as the epistemically central, default method for understanding other agents. . . . (Stueber 2006: 5)*

The concept of empathy, highlighting respectively "understanding" and "emotion," emerged through the convergence of two philosophical traditions at the turn from the nineteenth to the twentieth century. From the perspective of aesthetics it was argued that the observer of a work of art could experience the emotion that inspired the artist through "aesthetic empathy" (Lipps 1912–1913). On the other hand, philosophical hermeneutics sought to gain insight into the author's meaning in a text through "empathic understanding" (Heidegger 1962). In each case the inner meaning of phenomena is communicated through the medium of an external object. In her doctoral thesis, "On the Problem of Empathy," Stein describes how in empathy we are given internal experiences of the emotions of others, emotions which nevertheless require work on our part to differentiate.

> *When it arises before me all at once, it faces me as an object (such as the sadness I "read in another's face"). But when I enquire into its implied tendencies (try to bring another's mood to clear givenness to myself), the content, having pulled me into it, is no longer really an object. I am now no longer turned to the content but to the object of it, am at the subject of the content in the original subject's place. And only after successfully executed clarification does the content again face me as an object. (Stein 1916: 10)*

Stein identifies the dynamic move from objectively observing the other's emotion towards an internal subjective experience of that emotion. Only after a process of "clarification" can distance be re-established with a return to objective observation. She goes on to argue that this is in fact the natural way of things:

> *Without doubt, our ability to understand other people as minded creatures in this way has to be conceived of as the psychological foundation of our ability to be social animals and to become full members of society. (1916: 11)*

Other writers have contributed to our understanding of empathy. For example, Bion (1959) suggests that empathy is a necessary and healthy aspect of projective identification, fulfilling a communicative function of giving the other an experience of what self is like. Unlike pathological projective identification, there is no "loss of reality or confusion of identity" (Hinshelwood 1989). Greenson, too, emphasized the centrality of empathy for understanding others and particularly for therapists' insight into their patients' dilemmas:

> One cannot truly grasp subtle and complicated feelings of people except by this 'emotional knowing'. It is 'emotional knowing', the experiencing of another's feelings, that is meant by the term empathy. It is a very special mode of perceiving. Particularly for therapy, the capacity for empathy is an essential prerequisite. (1960: 418)

These writers stress two important considerations within the "process framework" for supervision which I have outlined. Firstly, empathy is a natural process through which we come to know others. In fact, empathic exchange occurs without any effort on our part unless it is seriously restricted in conditions like autism or psychopathy. Secondly, empathy as a primary mode of knowledge generation is not predicated on prior knowing. Hence it marks the beginning of the process framework and is prepared for by suspension of any previous knowledge.

However, while emotional knowing is our primary way of knowing self and others, there is a price to pay. If the client feels murderous rage, paralyzing fear, or dark depression, for example, then the supervisee too will feel murderous rage, paralyzing fear, or dark depression. Stern (2002) was acutely aware of the dangers posed by empathic resonance:

> We are born with the capacity . . . to experience what others experience and participate in their experience by virtue of the way we are grabbed by their nervous system. One of the real questions is not, "How in the world does this happen?" We're beginning to have a really good idea. The real question is "How do we stop it from happening so that we are not the prisoner of someone else's nervous system," and probably that will be a very interesting area of research which has not been addressed so far. (Quoted in Rothschild 2006: 9)

The risk of being overwhelmed by the feelings of the other is particularly real in the case of high impact settings such as residential childcare, trauma, mental health, abuse, and emergency services, among others. Burnout, secondary traumatization, vicarious traumatization, and compassion fatigue will become familiar to these practitioners (Rothschild, 2000, 2002, 2006).

2. Phase Two: Presentational and Propositional Knowing

> *Jessica opened the next supervision session with the following words: "You will think this is terrible of me and I know I shouldn't have felt this way. I just couldn't help it, I was just so mad at him. After all the work I have been doing trying to be open to him the wee b...... just spits in my face. It was all I could do not to punch him in the face in return. Now I know why no one else wants to work with him. I just can't have any empathy for him. I'm not cut out for this job and I knew I shouldn't have come here. This always happens to me."*

Stueber (2006) has argued that "empathy must be regarded as the epistemically central, default method for understanding other agents." Despite this it is not unusual for supervisees with words like Jessica's to preface acknowledgment of intense emotions aroused by a client. The supervisees assume that feeling rage is somehow wrong. Often this feeling is exacerbated by professional judgments that they have become over-involved or are taking it all too personally. So often supervisees have been shamed into denying that they have strong emotional reactions to their clients. Supervision facilitates presentational knowing that allows, within a permissive environment, the experience to be brought into the room. Drawing on propositional knowledge about empathy enables supervisees to understand that they might feel the way they do because they are doing something right rather than something wrong. Intense feelings of rage might indicate an accurate empathic resonance with the clients' intense rage. What is construed as loss of empathy might better be expressed as a struggle to maintain sight of "unconditional positive regard" or "therapeutic neutrality" while lost in the mists of empathic turmoil or countertransference mayhem. In response to the emotional turbulence, Jessica is driven to consider the precipitous solution of leaving her job.

Rothschild (2000, 2002, 2006) has given much thought to the ways in which empathic impact can be managed and contained. Acknowledging its ubiquitous presence and recognising its crucial nature as a primary source of supervisees' knowledge of clients' dilemmas, she draws on contemporary neuroscience to locate empathy within the motor division of the autonomic nervous system. Since the motor division is about action, perhaps we ought not be so surprised when supervisees experience intense empathic impact from clients. Often their first instinct is to act, to do something about it. On the contrary, presentational knowing is about facilitating a creative space in a learning environment that values reflection on the empathic encounter leading to informed action. The process framework facilitates slowing down the natural urgency for action. At times, this requires extreme effort. The development of emotional intelligence that results from this process facilitates transformational learning by enhancing the capacity for the supervisee's "emotional and intellectual growth" (Casper 2001: 17).

> Jessica was encouraged to bring into the supervisory conversation the full emotional impact Brian had on her. At this point we were unconcerned about any information from Brian's case history about his family life or care. Our hunch was that all of his emotional pain was being communicated with Jessica in the here and now. That pain is captured in the sub-text of her rage as he spat on her. Gradually she unpacks the depth of the emotion, recognizing some of it as familiar to her as she grew up ("this always happens to me") and some that seems strange to her ("but I don't usually give up like this"). Jessica began to distinguish sympathy from empathy, sympathy being the set of emotions that arose in her from her own experience of rejection as she is moved "for" Brian. Empathy, on the other hand, consists of the set of emotions that arose when she was moved "by" Brian's rage.

There may be issues identified here that belong to unresolved conflicts for Jessica and we don't assume that the most distressing element of the emotional exchange comes from Brian. If this is the case, over time Jessica can begin to identify patterns of emotion within herself that may limit her capacity to work effectively. A wide range of clients may evoke similar rage and the meaning of this for Jessica would need to be attended to in some place other than supervision. In the meantime, as a supervisor, I facilitate learning by providing a space for creative exploration of the empathic experience, an experience whose meaning Jessica makes from her theoretical perspective as a social worker.

> As a social worker, Jessica had been helping Brian complete a "life-book" as he recalled his experiences of growing up in a disturbed family. Jessica now began to read the life-book and the case notes in his file through the lens of the rage she felt rather than the lens given her by others; that is, the expectation that he was going to make a complaint against her. She looked at the relationships in his life and imagined what it would be like if the rage she felt was something like how he felt in relation to all these people, although he was unable to understand or say anything about it. Perhaps what Brian couldn't say was that he felt not-good-enough to be a son, brother, or friend, just as she had felt not-good-enough to be a social worker. She began, through her theoretical perspective, to reframe the experience with him as a communication to her rather than an attempt to reject her. She wondered then if this clumsy communication was what led all the others to reject him.

The dynamic of empathy means that clients will recreate their style of emotional relatedness with all those with whom they interact. Differences between relationships will be reflective of a fragmented sense of self, some idealized and some denigrated. We expect these emotions to be re-enacted in stressful situations with professional helpers. However, an important difference between the helping relationship and others in the clients' lives is that professional helpers bring theoretical perspectives from which to understand the patterns of relationship. Many supervisees, aware of the centrality of the relationship for effective outcomes (Roth and Fonagy 2005), resist turning towards theory to help understand what is happening. This may be because they undervalue theory or because they lack confidence in working with the theory. I suspect it is often because supervisees have not been encouraged during their professional training to embrace emotions through their theory and "think-feelingly."

Propositional or theoretical knowing constitutes the lens through which supervisees reflect on the emotional impact their clients have on them, allowing the encounter to be understood from a different perspective. In this case, Jessica can begin to hear what could only be communicated by spitting and her reflection opens up a whole new perspective on Brian's life story. It is often at the point of applying theory that supervisees can have transformational moments of insight: "So that might be what is happening. Maybe I'm not such a bad social worker after all." The reduced stress level frees up the supervisees' capacity to think creatively and reflect at increasingly deeper levels about their clients' dilemmas. Propositional knowing enhances the insights gained through emotional knowing, as Greenson says: "empathy and theory complete each other" (quoted in Bolognini 2004: 48). The supervisor brings the generic propositional knowledge of learning and knowledge development while supervisees bring their specific theories of professional practice. If supervisees are in training, and have not yet consolidated a practical awareness of their underpinning theory, then it is important that the supervisor be able to offer a grounding in that theoretical perspective.

If, as Greenson has suggested, empathy and theory do complete each other, it is at the service of more richly informing, practical interventions.

3. Phase Three: Purposeful Application of Knowledge

Jessica continued in supervision: "If Brian is feeling the kind of impotent rage that I was feeling then how can I let him know at an emotional level that I understand something of what he is feeling. It is important for me not to retaliate, as I felt inclined to do when I wanted to hit him and incur a complaint against me, or collapse, as I felt inclined to do when I wanted to pack the job in." Jessica begins to think about what Brian needs from her as a result of her insights into his rage. She is no longer boiling and can bring a different emotional presence to him at the next opportunity.

Many programs for counselors begin by introducing trainees to the skills of counseling, putting these in a theoretical context and then recommending personal work to enhance self-awareness. In contrast, the process framework argues that practical intervention skills best emerge from the insights of emotional self-awareness and propositional knowing. Thinking-feelingly can yield the capacity to act-feelingly-with-insight. The process framework provides something akin to what Bion (1959) described as containment. The clients' hot emotions are soothed through empathic holding, giving emotional quality to the words that supervisees use in response. In a similar way the reflexive space of supervision gives the supervisee an opportunity to practice trial interventions prior to their next encounter with the client (Casement 1985). Over time this process makes the internal supervisor more robust. However, the bridge between supervision and re-entry into the next professional encounter presents another challenge requiring a new level of suspension on the part of the supervisee.

While supervisees are engaging in reflexive processes, their clients have continued on their relational journeys. What clients bring to the next encounter will differ from what they carried away when they left the previous one. Once again, blindly implementing insights gained through reflection in supervision leaves supervisees without an ability to see subtle changes in their clients' emotional experience. I think this is one of the trickiest steps in the whole process. I recall one powerful experience many years ago when my own supervisor formulated what I thought was an absolutely brilliant and accurate interpretation of my client's internal world and I set off excitedly to apply it at the next session. Awaiting my opportunity I eventually offered the intervention, which simply did not sit with the material of the moment. The client raised her head from what was quite a depressed state and with a broad grin on her face said, "You got that in supervision, didn't you?" We both laughed.

Interventions that lack emotional connection to the moment sound robotic and bookish. Lacking any sense of emotional quality, conviction, or understanding, they leave clients and practitioners unmoved. Rather than formulations and interventions, supervisees bring to the next encounter an altered emotional state—that Stein (1916) refers to as "reiterative empathy"—that indicates a fresh emotional knowing. Reiterative empathy is the process by which we learn about ourselves through empathic resonance with the other's experience of us and this becomes a crucial component of our grounding as human:

. . through reiterated empathy I become aware of myself as others are aware of me and so understand my physical body as one and the same as the living body of my lived experience. And so it is that I am for the first time given to myself as "a psychological individual in the full sense."
(Macintyre 2006: 83)

Stein (1916) has argued that empathy provides our best insights into how others are as human beings and, unsurprisingly, it has become the dominant therapeutic tool for counselors and therapists. It is also, but less recognized as such, the key tool for insight by any helping professional, as it was for Jessica the social worker. All practitioners, regardless of professional orientation, will resonate with their clients' emotions. A key factor of therapeutic outcome will be how they manage and process that emotional impact. Reiterative empathy is the emotional component of the professionals' interventions, offering clients an empathic awareness of how they are experienced. This, for example, is how rescue workers or paramedics comfort crash victims while they are being cut from the wreckage. Unfortunately, reiterative empathy is as natural as empathy. It bypasses demeanor, making it impossible for supervisees to hide how they feel from their clients who will be intensely sensitive to their emotional state. Finding the right emotional language that is true to the feelings is crucial for the communication of understanding.

"When I met Brian again I was no longer full of rage, no longer full of shame at my own feelings and no longer convinced that I was not a good social worker. Carrying these feelings about myself, I wanted to let him know that I no longer experienced him as a dangerous person, as someone I needed to protect myself from, and that he did not need to be ashamed of his need for others. I did this by exploring with him how he felt in many of the instances of his life story that he shared with me. Together we re-wrote the life-book, this time at a deeper level of understanding."

A much richer emotional narrative became possible when Jessica used reflexive processes to experience, understand,

and use the communication of empathic resonance that
for so long in Brian's life had led to further rejection.

Conclusion

We are in a new era of cross-professional supervision, exemplified
in this instance by a supervisory relationship between Jessica the social
worker supervisee and me, as her supervisor, with a background in
contemporary object relations psychoanalytic psychotherapy. While I
didn't jettison my knowledge of psychology, the primary knowledge I
brought to the relationship was a philosophy of learning and a process
framework that facilitated reflexivity. Jessica brought her experience
of Brian, her knowledge of social work practice, and in particular the
practical exercise of the life-book. Brian brought the life dilemmas
that he needed help to understand and change. Supervisors provide
non-shaming environments in which learning is possible. The process
framework explored here gives supervisors a set of tools for encouraging
just such environments.

Gadamer (1975) has described the task of hermeneutics as one not
of defining the procedure of understanding but rather one of attending
to the conditions in which understanding can emerge from experience.
He might profitably be paraphrased in reference to the learning
environment of supervision as follows: the work of supervision is not
to develop a procedure of learning, but to facilitate the conditions in
which learning can take place.

Bibliography

Alonso, A. 1985. *The Quiet Profession: Supervisors of Psychotherapy*. London: Macmillan.

Alvesson, M. and Skoldberg, K. 2000. *Reflexive Methodology*. London: Sage.

Assagioli, R. 1985. *The Act of Will*. Wellingborough: Turnstone Press.

Bion, W. 1959. "Attacks on Linking." *Int. J. Psycho-Anal.*, 40: 308–15.

Bion, W. 1976/1994. "Evidence." In W. R. Bion. *Clinical Seminars and Other Works* ed., F. Bion. London: Karnac.

Bolognini, S. 2004. *Psychoanalytic Empathy*. London: Free Association Books.

Casement, P. 1985. *On Learning from the Patient*. London: Routledge.

Casper, C. M. 2001. *From Now On with Passion: A Guide to Emotional Intelligence.* Fort Bragg, CA: Cypress House.

Carroll, M. 1996. *Counselling Supervision: Theory, Skills and Practice.* London: Cassell.

De Bono, E. 1996. *Thinking Course: Powerful Tools to Transform Thinking.* London: Henry Ling.

Gadamer, H. G. 1975. *Truth and Method* trans. P. Siebeck. New York: Sheed and Ward. Quoted in G. Burns. 1992. *Hermeneutics Ancient and Modern.* New Haven: Yale University Press: 12.

Gilbert, M. and Evans, K. 2000. *Psychotherapy Supervision: An Integrative Approach to Psychotherapy Supervision.* Buckingham: Open University Press.

Greenberg, J.R. and Mitchell, S.A. 1983. *Object Relations in Psychoanalytic Theory.* Cambridge: Harvard University Press.

Greenson, R. 1960. "Empathy and Its Vicissitudes." *Int. J. Psycho-Anal.*, 41:418–424.

Greenson, R. 1967. *The Technique and Practice of Psychoanalysis.* London: Hogarth Press.

Hawkins, P. and Shohet, R. 2000. *Supervision in the Helping Professions,* 2nd ed. Buckingham: Open University Press.

Heidegger, M. 1927. *Being and Time,* trans. J. Macquarie and E. Robinson. 1962. New York: Harper & Row.

Hinshlewood, R. D. 1989. *A Dictionary of Kleinian Thought.* London: Free Association Books.

Holloway, E. 1995. *Clinical Supervision: A Systems Approach.* London: Sage.

Kolb, D. A. 1984. *Experiential Learning.* Englewood Cliffs, NJ: Prentice-Hall.

Lipps, T. 1912–1913, in K. R. Stueber (2006). *Rediscovering Empathy: Agency, Folk Psychology and the Human Sciences.* Cambridge: MIT Press.

Macintyre, A. 2006. *Edith Stein: A Philosophical Prologue.* London: Continuum.

Mahrer, A. R. 2004. *Theories of Truth, Models of Usefulness: Towards a Revolution in the Field of Psychotherapy.* London: Whurr Publishers.

Moore, R. M. 2005. "The Centrality of the Empathic Relationship with Clinical Supervision." *British Journal of Psychotherapy Integration*, Vol. 2, Issue 1.

Moore, R. M. 2008. *Group Supervision with a Multi-Disciplinary Trauma Resource Team in the North of Ireland: A Participative Inquiry into the Application of a "Process Framework" for Supervision.* Middlesex: Metanoia Institute/Middlesex University doctoral study.

Page, S. and Wosket, V. 1994. *Supervising the Counsellor: A Cyclical Model.* London: Routledge.

Reason, P. and Bradbury, H. 2001. *Handbook of Action Research.* London: Sage.

Roth, A. and Fonagy, P. 2005. *What Works for Whom? A Critical Review of Psychotherapy Research,* 2nd ed. London: Guildford Press.

Rothschild, B. 2000. *The Body Remembers: The Psychophysiology of Trauma and Trauma Treatment.* New York: Norton.

Rothschild, B. 2002. *"Case Studies: The Dangers of Empathy."* *Psychotherapy Networker*, Vol. 16, No. 4.

Rothschild, B. 2006. *Help for the Helper: A Psychophysiology of Compassion Fatigue and Vicarious Trauma.* London: Norton.

Schön, D. 1996. "From Technical Rationality to Reflection-in-Action." *Boundaries of Adult Learning.* eds. R. Edwards, A. Hanson and P. Raggatt. London: Routledge.

Senge, P., Scharmer, O., Jaworski, J. and Flowers, B. 2005. *Presence: Exploring Profound Change in People, Organisations and Society.* London: Nicholas Brealey Publishing.

Scharmer, C. O. 2007. *Theory U: Leading from the Future as it Emerges.* Cambridge: Society for Organisational Learning.

Stein, E. 1989. "On the Problem of Empathy." In *The Collected Works of Edith Stein,* trans. W. Stein. Vol. 3. Washington: ICS Publications.

Stern, D. N. 2002. "Attachment: From Early Childhood Through the Lifespan." In B. Rothschild. (2006). *Help for the Helper: A Psychophysiology of Compassion Fatigue and Vicarious Trauma.* London: Norton.

Strachan, D. 2007. *Making Questions Work.* San Francisco: Jossey-Bass.

Stueber, K. R. 2006. *Rediscovering Empathy: Agency, Folk Psychology and the Human Sciences.* Cambridge: MIT Press.

PART III

Integrating Practice and Theory

CHAPTER

11

❧

A Conversation with Robin Shohet

❧ *Geraldine Holton* ❧

The gift of this conversation arose when, as Chair of the Supervisors Association of Ireland (SAI), I contacted Robin Shohet to explore the possibility of Robin presenting at the next SAI conference. From our first conversation I sensed a resonance with his vision of supervision, particularly around the emerging practice of cross-professional supervision and our mutual interest in spirituality and supervision. This experience prompted me to invite Robin to contribute to a text I was co-editing with Margaret Benefiel entitled *The Soul of Supervision*. Robin suggested that we take a conversational style and trust the process. And so we did.

Robin is a co-founder of the Centre for Supervision and Team Development (www.cstd.co.uk) which has been training supervisors for over thirty years. For the last sixteen years he has been living with his family in the Findhorn spiritual community in Scotland.

I hope this conversation will allow the insights and uniqueness of Robin to enrich and develop our understanding of supervision. Robin's wisdom, fired (linking with his book *Passionate Supervision*) through personal commitment and reflective practice, is clearly challenging and innovative.

☙❧

Geraldine Holton: *Robin, in a fast-changing, busy world,* reflection *and* silence *are key practices, but many practitioners find them difficult. Are they key practices for you in supervision, and if so, why do you feel they are important?*

Robin Shohet: I am going to be talking as a group supervisor and trainer which is where I do most of my work. I start all of my groups by saying that my intention is to go as slowly as I can, that the world is pushing us into needing quick answers, that there is very little space for not knowing, for waiting. So I guess the answer to your question is yes, they are key practices, although I use the terminology "going as slowly as I can." I model this by pausing quite a long time before giving an answer, sometimes just waiting. I don't set aside separate times for meditation because the whole experience for me is a meditation.

There is another aspect to your question and this will take us into another place altogether. There is a well-known saying that today's problems are a result of yesterday's solutions. This usually strikes a chord with people. If we examine this, then the quick fix does not usually go to the root of the problem but just alleviates the immediate symptoms. As such the problem will reoccur, perhaps in an even worse form because the so-called solution was not a solution at all and now the situation has become even more complex.

GH: *Yes, Robin, there is apparent safety in answers and solutions which as you say are not really solutions at all. I find it much more challenging to slow down and be with the questions, the deeper questions I am being invited to reflect on. That brings us into the space where vulnerabilities can be uncovered and released so that what research names as "hiding" in supervision can be revealed.*

In your writing on passionate supervision you reflect on this aspect when you say that you sometimes begin your training by asking people to write what they would least like people to know about their work. Can you say a little more about this?

RS: Well, my view is that we humans are weird creatures. We deeply want to be seen, to be known, and at the same time spend enormous amounts of energies hiding. My job is to create an environment where the need to hide is less. I ask people to write answers to the question, "What would you least like your supervisor to know about your work?" I promise them that they will not need to share those answers. I then ask them to finish the sentence. "I would be reluctant to share this because. . . ." I ask them to share the reasons, which usually amount to: I would look stupid, or I would be seen as not knowing the answer, or I might be judged. Most people in the group can identify with the reasons and suddenly they are shown to be not so important and then people often voluntarily share the content, the answer to the first question, with tremendous relief and laughter. Some of the biggest taboos are feeling murderous towards clients, being bored by them, or fancying them. These feelings are often a source of shame to practitioners and because of this they may be reluctant to share them with their supervisor. I want to create a climate, free of judgment, where supervisees can use all their feelings as information, so we can explore together from where these feelings might possibly arise.

I want to normalize the big taboos, to not make them a source of shame which causes people to hide. You know there is a big deal about differences: race, gender, class, etc. Without underestimating those differences, I want to get to the bit where we are all the same—aware of our mortality, our imagined separation, our fears of getting old, and losing the ones we love. So I use the idea of what we would least like to share about our work as a starting point. And I want to be clear; I never push anyone to share. It is not my interest. I find that people want to share when they realize they are not alone with their fears.

GH: *Perhaps we all walk around with some feeling of "not good enough"—a feeling of lack of being which contributes to the "hiding."*

Reflecting on group supervision, many say that a group setting is a key limitation because individuals have more opportunities for hiding in group. What you say really challenges this whenever people realize they are not alone with their fears. I can see the importance of group for this move towards freedom.

Can you say a little about group, another important aspect of supervision?

RS: Groups can be an incredible source of support or potential persecution. My paramount job is to create safety. Of course there are many ways in which I create safety, non-verbally and implicitly, but also explicitly when I ask for a goodwill contract, which is more than confidentiality but includes it. Confidentiality has fear attached to it. By goodwill I mean that no one says anything that could potentially hurt or be disrespectful to another. We are here to support each others' learning, to create a learning community, and knowing we are there for each other is very important, which is why I need everyone's goodwill to make a group work. Confidentiality does not go far enough for me. Goodwill refers to creating a learning community which includes respect for all, including the client.

The feeling of "not good enough" is almost universal by the way. And this is another point I can enlarge; how in one way we are all frauds. I can sound very wise as I sit here, but the reality is I can be full of irrational fears and anger. The more I am open about this, the more "good enough" I feel because I am not wasting energy hiding. And the group can really help with this because, when it is working well, there is very little hiding and there is a sense of relief when we discover how similar we all are in having the thought of not being good enough.

GH: *I really connect with the idea of a goodwill contract. Through this dialogue a new awareness has emerged for me about taking time to* notice from where *questions and concepts such as "hiding" or "confidentiality" arise. Are they rooted in love or fear? In practice we are often in fear mode.*

Creating a learning community which includes respect for all allows room for the revelatory, generative aspect of supervision to emerge, particularly in a group.

Through my experience as Director of the MA program in supervisory practice, I have come to value the learning community in which participants are invited to bring their whole selves—body, mind, heart, and soul—which creates an invitational space for transformation. Can you suggest what enables this generative aspect, the soul of supervision, to come alive within the supervisory process?

RS: Well, tell me what you do?

GH: *Grounded in a contemplative tone, I invite the learning community to come into the present and to receive who and how they are at each moment without criticism or judgment, just to notice and receive and share from that space. Whenever all aspects of body, mind, heart, and soul are included, I find most people are thirsting for a safe space in which they can uncover that meaning-making aspect, the authentic voice within. I try to facilitate that process and feel privileged as a reflective witness within this revelatory, generative space of supervision.*

I am interested in hearing your thoughts on how as a supervisor you may encourage the soul of supervision to come alive within the supervisory process?

RS: I am not sure what is meant by the soul of supervision as it is not a term I use. What I would say is that I am interested in going beyond mind, beyond ego, and beyond fear. Behind all of those is love. So my job is to deconstruct as many limiting, fear-based ideas as I can. It is extraordinary how conditioned we all are on such topics as suicide, illness, and damage. In the first chapter of *Passionate Supervision*, Jochen Encke talks about going beyond stories and thinking outside the box as he challenges our thinking about even some of the most extreme stories of suffering. It is a brilliant chapter. He talks about soul a lot. The only reason I don't use it is that it is too vague for me, but you could equally turn to me and ask how do you know love is behind everything and I could not prove it. Love, soul—in the end I don't object to either term.

GH: *From our earlier conversation Robin, you know how passionate I am about trying to understand and engage in cross-professional supervision. It is a challenge to move outside the boundaries of the accepted uni-professional understanding of supervision to become a supervisor from a different discipline working with a supervisee. Can you say a little about how you understand supervision?*

RS: I have supervised people in most of the helping professions and our courses always have had a huge mix—from people working in the fire service to police, probation officers, nurses, OTs doctors, youth workers, counselors, therapists, and coaches. They almost always report that they enjoy hearing about each other's work. There are times when my not knowing about a profession can be a handicap but that will usually be obvious. One Chief Executive said to me, "If I want something that relates to the operational side of things, I go elsewhere. But you take me beyond that, to a place where I can question, go outside my usual frames of reference." I can also draw analogies from the Inner Game to describe aspects of awareness. For example, in the *Inner Game of Tennis* the mind is given something to occupy itself with—shouting "bounce" when the ball bounces and "hit" when the racquet makes contact. The body then just gets on and hits the ball without any mental interference, such as, "I am not good enough, my backhand isn't working, or do I have my feet in the right position?" The techniques are applicable to any sport. I coached a golfer, never having played golf in my life. By helping to remove the mental chatter (I'm not good enough, etc.), we were creating the conditions to let the body wisdom emerge. I did not need to know the technicalities of golf. I can also ask questions like, "How do you know when you have hit a good shot?" and then ask, "How can you do more of that?" Asking good questions allows the body to do the work in sport, and the unconscious do it in supervision. In supervision we can help supervisees find their own answers with questions like, "If you knew the answer, what would it be? Or what is stopping you from knowing what to do? Or if you could do or say anything you wanted, what would it be?" These are questions which help to bypass the critical mind and enable the supervisee to move to a new level of awareness. On the one hand, the example seems to be that you occupy or distract the mind from thinking too much (say "hit" so the mind doesn't say, "My backhand is lousy.") On the other hand, you are saying that the right questions provoke more self-awareness.

GH: *As a supervisor and a reflective practitioner I am challenged to cultivate an open, curious mind, a sense of wonder. Yet it is more than this; it is also wondering about the political and social structures which are increasingly oppressing professionals. An area that I currently wonder about and find confining is the whole area of accreditation. It is a real challenge to find a balance between accountability and conformity. How can we support and challenge otherwise credible, responsible, and accountable practice without merely conforming to minimum requirements and in the process missing the transformational opportunity available to a learning community? I am searching for a way that leads to real freedom and growth. How do you navigate the stormy seas of accreditation?*

RS: Well, this is a long answer. Twenty years ago, I was very worried about what I could see happening. I organized two conferences to look at the dynamics of accreditation—not to fight it, but just to understand. We did a simulation during which we gave tokens to clients, therapists, supervisors, and trainers and it became clear that the more conditions that were required, the more money went to the trainers. So it seemed to be more about money than protecting the client. Of course that was just a simulation, but there was some truth to it.

Now I have been a trainer for thirty years and I had an ethical dilemma as I did not want to create a big training body which asked people to jump through lots of hoops, but at the same time unless we did something no one would attend our courses. We in fact give a certificate, based on self- and peer-assessment, but we have not sought outside accreditation for our courses. We would like to think we have found a middle way. Occasionally people who are initially interested drop out when they hear we are not accredited, but we have survived for thirty years with almost no advertising. We really believe in self-direction and so we try and embody that as much as possible. By the way, out of these conferences came the Independent Practitioners Network (IPN). This network involves small peer groups that self- and peer-assess, and who elect representatives to visit each others' groups to give feedback and to provide some kind of accountability. To some of the people I trained here, I suggested organizing a conference in Ireland to look at the dynamics of accreditation, but there seemed very little interest. There are big issues here revolving around fear and trust which go far beyond accreditation.

GH: *Your long but* hope-filled *answer to my question encourages me to keep thinking outside the box. Your journey on the stormy sea reminds me of the Celtic pilgrims heading out to sea in their little boat (coracle) without oars, trusting the journey. Perhaps if the process of quality assurance in supervision were more trusting and focussed on developing an effective "internal supervisor," supervision would become less of a monitoring process and more a process of unfolding and uncovering a personal philosophy of supervision grounded in a personal belief system and a professional ethical system. Bolton describes this meta-stance as "the hawk in your mind constantly circling over your head watching and advising you on your actions—while you are practicing." I believe this approach could release latent creative resources in caring for the client. Have you any thoughts on developing the internal supervisor?*

RS: I like your metaphors. One of the things I keep going back to is awareness. I haven't read Tony de Mello for ages but I seem to remember he stresses this. When we really develop awareness, many of the things we have talked about are relevant—a reflective space, going slowly, a learning community, and goodwill. In my experience, these practices expose how much fear we carry and it is this fear which blocks awareness, takes us out of ourselves, and leads us not to trust ourselves and hence others. I think the internal supervisor and awareness might be the same thing. And this internal supervisor might encourage us to think and act in a very unconventional way, outside the box. The danger is that all this focus on accreditation can keep us inside the box.

GH: *Yes, can is appropriate as your experience has shown. This challenge also touches on the whole area of evaluation in supervision. I was curious to discover that many supervisors do not see this as a supervisory task or part of their role. As a supervisor I understand the supervisory process as a reflective learning space in which I am open to transformation and growth.*

By its very nature this evokes a collaborative approach to evaluation, where both supervisee and supervisor are open to give and receive feedback on a regular basis. This calls for real commitment to one another, to care enough to confront and challenge areas of strengths and limitations; it entails risk taking. Intentional reflective practice can engender transformative learning. As I struggle to construct a self-identity and a meaningful worldview, transformational learning in my experience is not easy because it invites me to face my defences, resistances, and avoidances. Could you expand on the transformation that occurs in your training and supervision groups? Does something similar happen in your groups?

RS: The transformation that really appeals to me is when the supervisee (or I) suddenly sees a whole new way of looking at an issue, a reframing that uncovers deeply held beliefs that may have been unconscious and are no longer deemed useful. Using an earlier example, I may respond to the question of what I would least like to tell my supervisor by saying, "I don't like this client." I don't want to share that response because I feel I should like my clients and I will feel judged. Is that true? Will I, as a supervisee, be judged? Well probably not. In fact, I am sure not. Oh my goodness. Of course I can tell my supervisor. The transformation is realizing that the rationalization is not true.

GH: *Transformational learning includes transcending the rational, widening the horizon, the vision. This is the core of supervision. Critical self-reflection (a term used in Transformational Learning Theory) on assumptions within a learning community of critical friends makes cross-professional supervision possible and desirable. Could you finish by returning to this theme? What do you see as the strengths and limits of cross-professional supervision?*

RS: It is interesting that you want to return to this. I would put it the other way round. Why on earth would there not be cross-professional supervision?

ᘒᕽᕽᗉ

This is a time of profound challenge and invitation, an exciting time to be a supervisor. One of the fruits of this conversation is that I have come to realize that I will not arrive at the answers to the challenges on my own, in fact I am not looking for answers but trying to uncover the right questions!

Robin's *quality of presence* and *reflective disposition*—which struck me in our first encounter—managed to shine through during our conversation. He has been a catalyst along the way, an agent of change, liberating others from fear. Through his quality of presence and care we have glimpsed the soul of supervision, what he names as love.

List of Contributors

Margaret Benefiel, Ph. D., has trained and supervised spiritual directors and currently focuses on supervision and spiritual direction in and for organizations. She teaches at Andover Newton Theological School in Boston and at All Hallows College in Dublin and serves as Executive Officer of ExecutiveSoul.com. She is the author of *Soul at Work* and *The Soul of a Leader*, as well as numerous articles.

Maureen Conroy, RSM, D.Min., has been educating spiritual directors and supervisors since 1982 at the Upper Room Spiritual Center, New Jersey, and at various places throughout the world. She wrote the first book on supervision of spiritual directors, *Looking into the Well: Supervision of Spiritual Directors*. Maureen is the author of many articles and four other books including *The Discerning Heart*.

Jack Finnegan, Associate Professor of Spirituality at the Milltown Institute in Dublin, teaches supervisory practice there. A founding member of the Supervisors Association of Ireland and founding chair of the National Association for Pastoral Counselling and Psychotherapy in Ireland, he presently chairs the All Ireland Spiritual Guidance Association. Author of *Audacity of Spirit: The Meaning and Shaping of Spirituality Today*, he has contributed to a number of edited collections in spirituality.

Geraldine Holton, a leading practitioner and trainer of psychotherapists, spiritual directors, and supervisors in Ireland and the United States, is currently engaged in doctoral research addressing cross-professional supervision. Chair of the Supervisors' Association of Ireland, she designed and directs an MA in Supervisory Practice at the Milltown Institute and All Hallows College in Dublin, and is the co-founder of An Croi Wisdom Learning Community, Drogheda.

Rev. Debora Jackson, M. Div., ME, MFE, MSM, is the Senior Pastor of the First Baptist Church in Needham, Massachusetts. Her calling to the pastorate has focused on congregational renewal and revitalization. She is also an independent consultant specializing in leadership development and organizational effectiveness.

Martin McAlinden is a priest of the Diocese of Dromore and has been in parish ministry for the past twenty years. He studied pastoral theology at Loyola University in Chicago which prepared him to work in adult faith formation. More recently he trained as a supervisor at the Milltown Institute in Dublin and currently offers pastoral supervision to clergy.

David McCormack is a lecturer in Adult and Community Education at National University of Ireland Maynooth. He works as a trainer and supervisor in a range of professional and organizational settings and is currently engaged in doctoral research at the University of Bristol on autoethnographic writing as an approach to reflective practice.

Robert M. Moore, DPsych, a registered psychoanalytic psychotherapist (ICP) and certified group psychotherapist (AGPA), works in private practice in Belfast. He offers leadership training, organizational consultancy, and retreats for Religious Congregations and Dioceses throughout Ireland and Britain. He also serves on the program team for the Doctorate in Psychotherapy at the Metanoia Institute, London.

Janet K. Ruffing, RSM, is professor in the practice of spirituality and ministerial leadership at Yale Divinity School. She is the author of *Uncovering Stories of Faith, Spiritual Direction: Beyond the Beginnings*, and editor of *Mysticism and Social Transformation*. She is one of the founding members of Spiritual Directors International and frequently leads workshops for spiritual directors.

Robin Shohet is co-author of *Supervision in the Helping Professions* (OU Press 2006, 3rd edition) and editor of *Passionate Supervision* (Jessica Kingsley Publishers 2007). He lives with his family at the Findhorn Foundation, a spiritual community in the North of Scotland. He has been coming to Ireland to teach since 1978 and it is still his favorite place to work.

Rev. Yuko Uesugi, M. Div., is the Director of ACPE Clinical Pastoral Education and Associate Director of the Spiritual Care Department at the UCLA Health System in Los Angeles, and has trained CPE Interns and Residents at the UCLA Health System. She is certified as a CPE Supervisor by the Association for Clinical Pastoral Education (ACPE) and ordained as an Elder by the United Methodist Church.

Index